DESIGNERS
DON'T
READ

AUSTIN
HOWE

D0104067

© 2009 Austin Howe

All rights reserved. Copyright under Berne Copyright Convention, Universal Copyright Convention, and Pan-American Copyright Convention. No part of this book may be reproduced, stored in a retrieval system, or transmitted in any form, or by any means, electronic, mechanical, photocopying, recording, or otherwise, without prior permission of the publisher.

14 13 12 11 10   6 5 4 3 2

Published by Allworth Press
An imprint of Allworth Communications
10 East 23rd Street, New York, NY 10010

Jacket, interior design, and typography by Fredrik Averin

ISBN: 978-1-58115-665-2

Library of Congress Cataloging-in-Publication Data:
Howe, Austin.
Designers don't read / written by Austin Howe ; designed by Fredrik Averin.
    p. cm.
ISBN 978-1-58115-665-2
1. Design. I. Title.
NK1510.H68 2009
745.4–dc22
2009019980

Printed in the United States of America

PALM BEACH COUNTY
LIBRARY SYSTEM
3650 Summit Boulevard
West Palm Beach, FL 33406-4198

*Reading times are estimated based on averages. Individual times may vary.

IF DESIGNERS DON'T READ, WHY DID I SPEND A YEAR WRITING THIS BOOK?

3.0 MIN.

This didn't start out as a book. It began as a series of essays sent out each week to a few of my favorite designers scattered throughout the country. Actually, it began with a profound sense of loneliness and alienation. After years in collegial and mostly invigorating work environments, I decided to scale back my operation, and I convinced myself that I was following in the footsteps of Paul Rand and Massimo Vignelli by building my own little dream studio in my own little dream home. The first few months were pure bliss, but I gradually began to realize that my wife Malinda actually had a pretty regular routine of her own that didn't necessarily allow for my periodic (and usually excitable) bursting in to share one of my regular epiphanies. So, I began to write them down and share them with anyone I happened to be working or dining with that day. Most of these designers and creative directors seemed to appreciate my perspective—a "bird's-eye view" of their professions as a passionate and semi-informed fan, student, advocate, colleague, and creative director. They began circulating these early essays to fellow designers and people within their firms, who forwarded them to their friends at other firms, and before I knew it, I had created the virtual version of an office full of extremely creative (and even influential) people expecting me to inspire or challenge them every Monday morning. I loved the inevitable and spirited feedback and interaction during the week. I had apparently struck a nerve, and eventually, I began to understand why: designers, if they're any good, are working. They're busy. And, with a few notable exceptions, they tend to be more visually oriented and more inspired by imagery than they are by words. Certain publishers have made their fortunes on this tendency. It's not that designers don't like to read or can't read. Quite the contrary; I find most designers to be very curious, informed,

13

and intellectual in their approach. It wasn't that I was sharing a lot of new concepts, either. Many of my readers had already studied or experienced many of the topics I was writing about—some in much greater depth than I had. But now, a few years into their careers, I think what they appreciated was a fresh, relevant context for those things, from someone who was not speaking as a design critic or (importantly) as a designer, but as a writer and creative director with an appreciation for—and a point of view about—design. Someone who had been in the trenches with them, but perhaps with a bit of distance or objectivity. (Or pure naiveté.) I also think that my experience in advertising provided designers with a portal into that world, and as the two worlds continued to converge at various points, I was able to help them navigate through some of the snares and pitfalls hidden there. Quite often, I found myself acting as an advertising Sherpa.

As you'll learn in my chapter about "How the Saarinen Family Saved Me from Becoming the Sausage King," I have long nursed a love and respect for design. My first boss at Cole & Weber said that I was the best art director of any writer he had ever worked with. Not that I ever tried to art direct or design, because I didn't. But I had a sense of what I liked and what seemed right. And I was very fortunate to be teamed with some very talented designers early on (my first project with Steve Sandstrom resulted in a One Show gold pencil).

By the time I moved into management, I had made design an important part of the creative process. Over time, I gradually did away with (advertising) art directors altogether, for reasons that will become obvious in "Designers versus Advertising Art Directors" and "Art Directors Don't Anymore," and opted to work only with smart, strategic designers. This decision, despite having provoked some head-scratching among my advertising peers, has resulted in the most rewarding and creatively satisfying period of my career. I have some very talented designers to thank for this, and *Designers Don't Read* is one small way of doing just that.

~~EVERY DESIGN FIRM SOUNDS~~ ~~EXACTLY THE SAME~~

3.5 MIN.

I finally figured out what was bothering me: every design studio in America speaks with exactly the same voice.

Okay, maybe that's a bit of an overstatement, but it's (almost) true. Try this: Write down a list of any five design firms and then go to their Web sites. That exercise alone should bring you pretty close to seeing my point; everyone has the obligatory "Clients," "People," "Process," "Philosophy," "Studio," "Contact," and my personal favorite, "News." But do what I just did and output the "Philosophy" bits. If you look at them with fresh eyes, you'll notice that the words themselves don't vary much from firm to firm, and the voice absolutely never varies. Oh, some sites are more wittily written than others. Some are more flip or irreverent. And some come across as pedantic, treating visitors as if they are complete novices when it comes to branding and design. (Maybe these firms assume that the only people visiting their sites are first-year design students.) But the voice of the copy—even for otherwise sophisticated design practices—comes from the exact same place with the exact same tone to (presumably) the exact same audience. I refer to it as the "infomercial voice," because it basically parallels a pitchman on late-night television who seems to be engaging only one audience: the potential, immediate shopper—people who certainly will be so impressed by all the features of this amazing product that they will naturally want to call the number on the screen right now and order. But wait—there's more!

This approach is known in sales circles as the "assumptive close," and I don't know about you, but when a salesman uses that tactic with me, my immediate reaction is flight; I am usually out of there in a hurry. But that's how most design firm sites talk to people: as though every visitor is a qualified client, and once all of the wonderful features of the

17

firm have been enumerated, that client is going to want to call or click "Contact" and start working with the firm immediately. In reality, any potentially great client relationship takes time to explore and nurture, but most of the people who are likely to visit their sites in the first place are probably not clients, and even fewer of them are potentially great (read: "qualified") clients.

The rhetoric on many of these sites is painful. I was going to cite some specific examples, and then thought better of it. (I want you to be inspired, not cranky.) I also decided not to go on a rant about quasi-proprietary Bullshit™ processes and methodologies that are probably no different from yours, except you just haven't "branded" them yet.

What is lacking (in my oh-so-humble opinion) is humanity. A human point of view, a real voice of a real person or persons, talking to me. Just once, I wish a design firm would speak in the first person. If the owner doesn't want to be thought of as the only designer in the studio, then they should have each of the designers write something (and hire me to edit). If nothing else, this will give potential clients a sense of the intelligence and wit of the people they might actually work with.

Personally, I prefer the "documentary voice," a third-party approach that is potentially even more powerful if a credible third party is doing the speaking. If I were Bruce Mau, I would ask Rem Koolhaas to talk about my firm's philosophy. If I were Stefan Sagmeister, I would ask Lou Reed to describe my company's process. And so on.

Speaking of Sagmeister, I also wish that design firms would tailor different sites to different audiences. Sagmeister's "Student" page is the closest I've seen to that.

18

(Also check out Sandstrom Partners' Web site—it was constructed specifically for different types of clients.)

Here's the irony: some of the most interesting, articulate, and inspiring people I know are designers, but you'd never reach that conclusion by looking at their Web sites.

"Advertising has to speak to everyone, and to do it quickly, it has only one chance of making itself heard, and that is the language of poetry."

— *A.M. Cassandre*

19

FINDING YOUR VOICE

4.5 MIN.

My hope is that design firms will become just a little more self-conscious about their branded communications, and, as a result of their heightened awareness, find their own unique "voiceprints" that no one else can duplicate.

Maybe the question is, "Is it even important for design firms to have their own voices?" Shouldn't they be invisible in a sense, and let the voices of the brands they work for come through? That would be an extremely compelling argument if design wasn't itself a business—an extremely competitive business. Besides, if design firms can't brand and differentiate themselves, how can they expect clients to trust that they can do it for them? It is almost axiomatic that design firms and advertising agencies are their own worst clients. Internal projects seem to fall to the bottom of the status sheet and get the lowest allocation of resources, both human and financial.

In theory, a design firm should be able to find its unique, differentiating voiceprint more easily than an advertising agency, just by virtue of its daily disciplines (e.g., organizing, editing and selecting information, moving freely from abstracts to concretes). Advertising agencies, by their very nature and function, are oriented more toward creation, addition, and compromise. An ad agency is more apt to come up with an idea and then add to it: directions, executions, media, client revisions. (David Ogilvy was right when he said that "most advertising people are flitting about on the surface of irrelevant brilliance." In my experience— to paraphrase a bumper sticker I once saw—designers drill deeper.)

Certainly, Wieden has a brand voice, maybe Crispin does, and so do KesselsKramer, Taxi, Mother, and Jung von Matt. But these are the exceptions. In a certain sense, Ogilvy and Chiat both have distinctive brand voices, but they are so large and spread out that their voices vary considerably across their multinational networks. Chiat was one of the first advertising agencies to take its own brand seriously. Mother rocked the advertising scene a couple of years back, not so much with the work it did for its clients, but because of how it positioned itself.

I have a couple of thoughts on how you can begin to discover your firm's unique brand voice.

First, take your key people aside (including yourself, since you're probably key) and ask them what one piece of art has had the greatest impact on them. "Art" can be defined as painting, sculpture, literature, or music. Most people have a hard time coming up with one piece, so tell them it doesn't have to be *the* piece, just one of the works that has impacted them. Then ask how or why it impacted them. I have been asking people this question for the past week or so, and the answers have been really interesting. I try to get to what it is about that piece, that song, or that book that resonates with them. I ask them to finish this sentence:

"It communicated the importance of _____ *."*

One of the pieces that has had the greatest impact on me is Picasso's *Les Demoiselles d'Avignon*. Quite apart from the fact that this was a revolutionary shot over the bow of hundreds of years of art history and the ushering in of Cubism (which I didn't know when I first saw it), it rocked my world because of its haunting mixture of intense beauty and sadness. It communicates the importance of looking past the suffering all around me to see "life's terrible richness." One piece that moved me so much that I had to buy it is a self-portrait collage of the artist Kris Hargis. It is

22

devastating in its vulnerability and sadness—he looks like he might be an emaciated AIDS victim—but it is also unbelievably beautiful. When I factor in my affinity for some of Damien Hirst's work and Rachel Whiteread's sculptures, a pattern begins to emerge that identifies something that is probably imprinted on my soul: *Look beyond the obvious. Don't be intimidated by suffering; find the beauty, find the joy and the sense of life.*

I am reading *The Romantic Manifesto* by Ayn Rand (no relation to Paul, despite the fact that her real name was originally Rosenbaum, which was also Paul Rand's surname). She posits that "man's profound need of art lies in the fact that his cognitive faculty is conceptual, i.e., that he acquires knowledge by means of abstractions and needs the power to bring his widest metaphysical abstractions into his immediate, perceptual awareness."

She argues that art concretizes our collection of abstract concepts and basically freezes one or two of them into a work that reveals something profoundly personal about the artist—and about ourselves. For Jim Riswold, who has broken new ground in the Dadaist tradition picking on malevolent dictators and despots, it boils down to an intensely personal experience of being intimidated by bullies (and possibly illness) and cutting them down to size by mocking and poking fun at them.

So, if you get bored and you want to stir things up a bit at your next staff meeting, pop the question and see what comes out. It might actually provide some clues as to what your firm is all about.

VOICE VERSUS STYLE

3.0 MIN.

Do you think your work has a particular quality to it that makes it uniquely yours? I think that might be okay.

Great writers have their own distinguishable voices, and no one criticizes them for bringing that same basic quality to each book they write—with slight variations and colorings. I've never heard anyone complain, "Dostoevsky uses the same voice in *Crime and Punishment* as he does in *The Brothers Karamazov*," or, "Hemingway only has one note." One voice, different *stories*.

I think designers (and artists) also have a voice. By voice, I don't necessarily mean "style" or "execution." Damien Hirst has a very unique, distinguishable voice, though his style and execution vary between installation, drawing, sculpture, and painting.

Hunter S. Thompson literally re-typed the entire manuscript of F. Scott Fitzgerald's *The Great Gatsby* just to see what it would feel like to write those words. I suspect that a few of my favorite designers have consciously or unconsciously mimicked other designers' voices at one time or another—just to see what it would feel like—before they discovered their own.

Even an extremist like me has a hard time completely peeling voice away from execution. Could we think of voice/style/execution as a gestalt, with voice being the most important part? Voice, in this context, implies content.

If ideas are primary, execution is secondary. The tools a designer uses to convey an idea are intended to serve the idea, the brief, and the brand. However, until software and robotics can start turning out successful

25

designs, there will be human beings (with minds and hearts and histories and biases and characters and tastes) creating the work. Remember the old adage that if you put enough monkeys in a room full of typewriters, they will eventually turn out the great American novel? Well, I've been watching the *New York Times* bestseller list for years, and so far, no monkeys.

The reason a company hires a design firm in the first place is generally for its unique "take" on the world. Or, more realistically, because that design firm has created work that has been successful *because* of its unique take on the world.

That view, I would argue, is the design firm's voice. In larger practices, there are (hopefully) several voices.

So, I guess my encouragement is this: If you're not 100 percent sure what your voice is, go back and study your favorite six or seven pieces that you've worked on and look for the threads. Jot down the qualities you notice when you look at them again. "Smart." "Witty." "Playful." "Evocative." "Respectful." "Ironic." "Simple." Whatever. If you can't be objective about it, ask someone else to do it. (Send them to me and I'll tell you what I see in your work.)

It's more likely that you already have a handle on your voice. I hear little snippets of negativity from time to time about certain designers' work having a particular look—criticism that often comes from other designers. However, this writer doesn't think you need to apologize for having a unique, distinguishable voice. It's what separates you from fully-automated design. And a roomful of monkeys.

~~DESIGN IS DRUMMING~~

2.0 MIN.

As a child, I was forced against my will to take piano and guitar lessons. At five years old, when the subject of drum lessons came up, I was all over it. The thought that I could actually beat the crap out of a drum with impunity seemed almost too good to be true—especially when Christmas rolled around and a sweet sparkle-blue drum kit was sitting by the tree.

I loved—and played—everything. Rock. Jazz. Blues. Even classical.

One of the highlights of my childhood was somehow finding myself sitting in the front row at a Buddy Rich concert at Disneyland. His left hand was faster than all of my appendages put together.

Here's my premise: As it relates to a design firm's relationship with its client, *the designer is the drummer.*

First of all, the design firm is absolutely crucial to the brand. The brand relies heavily on the design firm to provide a strong backbone that will keep that company's creative output all together, just like the drummer's groove keeps all the other instruments' parts together in a band. If the drummer/designer is weak, the whole band/brand will be weak

One of my musical heroes, Mickey Hart of The Grateful Dead, said that when he was a kid he thought that being a drummer was "more important than being the president." Having a sense of your firm's importance is not arrogance. It is actually crucial to you doing a good job for your client. Since the drummer provides the foundation for all of the other musicians to follow, you are the anchor of the band. The band will follow you—so you have to be competent, and you have to be confident. Confidence is what makes a good drummer a *great* drummer. And a great drummer

29

can actually make up for other musicians (clients) who may not be at the same level of expertise.

Obviously, the drummer is only one player in a larger band. Unless you're as good as Rich was, you probably won't be able to get away with being as difficult as he was. But valuing highly what you bring to the band, being solid, purposeful, strong, and confident—these are all necessary in order for your band, or your brand, to succeed.

Hart says, "We're living in a rhythm culture." To me, this implies that design's role in culture is more important now than ever.

ADDENDUM TO "DESIGN IS DRUMMING"

0.5 MIN.

In addition to keeping time and a steady tempo for the band, one of the most rewarding things about being a drummer is the freedom to do fills and the occasional solo.

Designers, please use this knowledge responsibly.

THE POWER OF THE POSTER

2.0 MIN.

Remember *School of Rock*, in which Jack Black's character, Dewey Finn, poses as a substitute teacher at an uptight private school and attempts to turn his class into a rock band? He shares with these fourth graders what amounts to his worldview:

"One great rock show can change the world."

Intuitively, we know this is true.

One other thing that I suspect most of us believe is that one great poster can change the world. There is just something about the gestalt of idea, type, and image, set in a public venue, that never seems to lose its power, regardless of the evolutionary effects of our increasingly digital existence. It almost seems that the poster was actually born for such a time as this, with our attention spans being auctioned off to the highest and most media-savvy bidder.

I find it particularly compelling how ancient a medium the poster is, its origins dating back to the prehistoric cave paintings of south-western France.

One of the most telling testaments to the enduring power of the printed poster is its political history. In 1653, the king of France felt that posters held too much power to create public fomentation and issued a decree forbidding the printing or displaying of posters—under penalty of death. Hmm. It is widely believed that Saatchi's "Labor Isn't Working" poster for the Conservative Party almost single-handedly defeated James Callaghan in 1978. It's often referred to as "the poster that won the election" for Margaret Thatcher.

I wonder if Paul Rand's clients at IBM lived long enough to see their "eye-bee-m" rebus poster sell online for $4,500. For one poster. With basically nothing on it but the company logo. (You can't get much more "viral" than having someone willing to pay thousands of dollars to have your logo on their wall.)

If some designers feel that the poster is a relic of the past, fine. That just means there's more opportunity for us. I say "us" because—as most of my favorite designers know—if there is a chance to create a great poster, I will happily waive my fee to work on it. Who wouldn't, for a chance to change the world?

PLANNERS, ACCOUNT PEOPLE, AND PROJECT MANAGERS

4.0 MIN.

First, an admission: I am a slave to account planning. I believe in it. I rely on it. And I have been fortunate enough to work with some of the best planners in the business. I am also aware that not everyone with "account planner" on his or her business card has the proper training, philosophy, or talent to inspire great work that's also on target. One of the best planners I've ever worked with asked me once, "Do you want me to lead you or just tee it up?" Damn. I didn't even know I had a choice. But this question not only changed how I viewed research, it made me trust this planner—deeply.

Great planners are consumer advocates, working with the manufacturer (us) to make sure that the consumer gets a great product. Their focus is on the consumer (their needs, wants, dreams, likes, and dislikes), and on making sure that the product (advertising, identity, packaging, etc.) connects with what they know about that consumer.

Great planners have a sense of boundaries and a respect for their team-mates (because if they are great, they're probably working at a place where the creatives are also great). They are there to lead, or to tee up. They are there to inspire. It's interesting: the better the planners, the more respect they seem to have for the creative process and for creative people themselves. Mediocre planners tend to be the ones who feel the need to step in and "help" the writers, designers, and art directors.

The most radical thing I ever heard a planner say was, "We do the best we can to lay it all out for the team, strategically; but if they get an inspiration that's off strategy, we change the strategy to fit the inspiration." This was from one of the most respected strategists in the world. The implication for my favorite designers is, make sure that the strategists

39

you work with understand their roles and also that they respect the roles of your other talented people. Bossy, meddling planners don't inspire trust or great work.

Account people: I can count on one hand (without using all of my fingers) the number of account people I would unhesitatingly refer to as "great." I'm sure there are more of them out there—I just haven't met them. The best one I have ever worked with (let's call him "Mike") had the following qualities: great taste, intelligence, huge heart, courage (read: "balls"), a sense of humor, and empathy (we nicknamed him "the priest"); he was a detail freak (this is key, because he was able to create a sense of confidence and trust with the client), and was seemingly on top of everything, and yet I don't think I ever heard him yell at anyone. His face just got really red. But here was the key to Mike's greatness: he had an artist in him. In college, he thought about a career as a writer or an art director, but ultimately decided that he'd make a better account person. This was a conscious decision, made with honesty and integrity. That initial impulse or drive that made him consider a career as a creative person settled somewhere deep in his soul, simmering and waiting for the next opportunity to make a great creative product come to life. He never once attempted to be a writer or an art director or a designer. Like planners who know the value of their roles as well as others', Mike knew the value of his role and the value of each individual member of the team. He also knew the value of planning. Most of all, Mike knew the value of a great creative product. I know what some of you are thinking: how can I get ahold of this guy, to hire him? Well, he's running an agency now and is hopefully spawning lots of other little Mikes.

40

To me, a great account person, like a great planner, realizes that we are in a product-driven, not a service-driven, business. A genius account person never lets his clients figure that out. The client feels that every concern, every risk, every contingency, every deadline and dollar is totally being managed with Germanic precision, that every angle has been considered (because it has), and that therefore, this crazy shit that we're presenting to them as a creative solution is as obvious as the nose on their face. I know there are other kinds of account people, and some of them probably do a fine job, depending on the system—usually where there is very strong creative leadership.

Project managers: I love them. Almost as much as I love account planners. In fact, based on my experience with most project managers at the design firms where I work, my vote would be to do away with account people altogether and just team up kick-ass planners with kick-ass project managers. (Oh, and there should probably be some kick-ass designers and writers in there, too.)

PLANNING AND DESIGN

8.0 MIN.

Okay, so I have a question:

What exactly is "graphic design," anyway? Or "communications design," if you prefer? (I personally prefer the latter, even though I'm about to propose a completely new descriptor for design practice—but we'll get to that in a bit.)

Is design primarily about aesthetics—about making things look great?

Is it primarily about style?

Is it about taste? Or typography? Or color stories? Or materiality?

Is it about "creativity" or "pushing the envelope"?

Or is it more about craft or craftsmanship?

Maybe design is best described as "creative problem solving." But isn't that simply a general description of the process within any of the applied arts, where a client and a budget and various other constraints present the actual problems to be creatively solved? Doesn't an architect, an interior designer, a fashion designer, an industrial designer, an illustrator, a photographer, or a commercial filmmaker solve problems with creativity?

It's possible that the field formerly known as graphic design is actually more about editing and the thoughtful ordering of information. If it is, why have I seen more and more clients and their design firms employing the services of "information architects" on big branding and Web projects? And what are those guys doing for their big, fat fees if not editing and ordering information?

43

Is a designer merely a *decorator*—someone who makes a writer's ideas and words more appealing and compelling (whether that "writer" is a proper writer with some degree of talent and craft, or a client or an account type person who is providing something aptly referred to as "copy")?

I said that I prefer the term "communications designer" to "graphic designer," for reasons that should be obvious—at least to the kinds of designers who are likely to read this. But I have a proposal for design firms who see themselves as more than decorators or illustrators. Or even rock stars.

I think great designers do more than solve visual problems. I think they do more than solve marketing problems. I think they are as capable of solving real world problems as they are of solving business problems, for one compelling reason: great designers create logical systems. Seriously—think about any major identity system that you have worked on. The degree of complexity and mental agility required to absorb all of the data points and constraints—from what is more often than not a disconnected and disparate collection of stakeholders—would be daunting even for an economist. And that's before you start developing a solution.

I define design as "beautiful logic." But I think a more accurate handle for any smart design firm, if it feels the need to differentiate itself from, say, interior designers or industrial designers, is "brand systems designers." You design brand systems. Brand logic. And the more holistic approach taken by the better design practices involves a complete and thorough assessment of a company's DNA, its soul—based on the beliefs and practices of the key stakeholders, its unique take on the world and on its category, as well as the brand's voice, look, and feel. All tangible expressions of the core of what a company or an organization is all about.

In that sense, there is no aspect or expression of that company that the designer doesn't influence in some way. That is, it's not one or two components of a company (like colors and typography) that a brand systems designer is concerned with, but every detail of that company's behavior and communications is viewed within the context of the whole: how that company treats and communicates with its employees, its suppliers, its community, and its customers. That requires a systemic approach. A complex, well researched, detailed, carefully considered analysis resulting in a logical, methodical, and realistic system and application of that system, followed by relentless attention to every detail of that company's brand. That is not about "graphics." That describes something much larger and more pervasive. That describes a system.

Theoretically, a C-level executive within a company or organization would own this. But owning and doing are completely different jobs, and even an inspired leader like Steve Jobs looks to Jonathan Ive and TBWA \ Chiat \ Day and Landor (or, in the case of his previous effort, NeXT, the brand systems designer of all brand systems designers, Paul Rand) to create and then keep their trained eyes on the (brand) ball: on the overall brand system.

So, I guess my encouragement to smart, strategic, ambitious "graphic designers" is this: stop thinking of yourself as a "graphic" designer, because if you are smart, strategic, and ambitious, you are most definitely designing more than "graphics." You are not just a "creative problem

45

solver," either, although that is no doubt a job requirement—as it is for your colleagues in architecture, interior, fashion, and industrial design, as well as commercial photographers, illustrators, and filmmakers. Hell, even writers have to solve problems with a degree of creativity sometimes.

Think bigger. Broader. Wider. Higher. Refuse to be thought of as a decorator, or worse, as a production artist—someone whose job it is to take someone else's ideas and make them look good.

As a designer, and as a design firm, insist on more.

The firms I see doing this are experiencing unusual success, while others suffer and shrink. JDK, based in Vermont with outposts in New York and Portland, is the poster child for brand systems design. It calls its approach Living Brand™, which I used to abuse it for, since the phrase smacks of that proprietary process Bullshit™ that many advertising and branding firms serve up for the sole purpose of creating a false sense of differentiation—usually for nervous mid-level marketing managers looking for an insurance policy for their jobs: "These guys have a Proprietary Process™…!" But the more I see from JDK, the more I realize that its process actually *is* different and that Living Brand™ is a pretty good way to describe it. JDK approaches a company or an organization or a concert like Ayn Rand's Howard Roark approached architecture:

"A building is like a man. It has integrity and just as seldom."

A company's brand is like a living person. Those people might very well need a specialist or two throughout their lives, but they also need someone who has a trained eye on the (health) ball: general practitioners with a holistic view toward the overall integrity of their patients' health.

46

JDK's own DNA is embedded in its very first success story: Burton Snowboards. The firm has been involved in virtually every aspect of that brand—and it shows. JDK's far-reaching and organic-bordering-on-spiritual approach has been repeated with each client. Some of the time, I suspect that it doesn't take (by virtue of a particular marketer's aversion to having a general practitioner). But most times it seems to work wonders—for the firm and for its clients.

This all brings me to my actual point about account planning or qualitative research—and design.

I myself am a slave to inspired research and fresh consumer insights, and, as an advertising person, there is nothing I covet, miss, or appreciate more than a single-minded, well crafted, inspiring, audacious strategy.

As an advertising person, not as a designer.

As I have collaborated with design firms and hybrid agencies over the past several years, I have observed an interesting development in terms of their attempts to integrate strategists and account planners into their creative processes. Namely, that it is a bit of an unnatural act. What has worked wonders for American advertising agencies since Jay Chiat imported the discipline from the U.K. in the early '80s has not proven to be equally as effective within design firms or hybrid firms that put design first. At least, not yet.

It's not that I don't think it can work; I just don't think it will work the same way that it works within an advertising agency, for one very simple reason: part of what makes a brand systems designer a *great* brand systems designer is something that can only happen during the process

47

of wrestling with the very things that most account planners and strategists wrestle with. If the strategist does all of that wrestling for the designer, it relegates that designer to being primarily focused on the execution of a preordained strategy. In other words, a decorator. To me, that's about the quickest way to take away the real value of any great designer.

Don't get me wrong: I am all for having as many smart, curious people in the room as possible. And I happen to believe that qualitative research is vital, if not mandatory for every major brand effort, and for many minor ones, as well.

I just think that any design-first firm that wants to avoid "decorator" status and move up and into a more holistic brand systems designer or trusted advisor role has to carefully consider and guard its creative process above everything else.

While collaboration should be encouraged, roles and specific boundaries need to be discussed, debated, and established—in short, adaptation. New systems will have to be established within these firms, and these systems should be driven and developed by the designers themselves. That is, after all, what they are good at: creating logical systems.

For years, during the height of Cahan & Associates' amazing success, the firm rarely hired strategists. Or writers. Instead, it established its business model on a point of differentiation: that it would "work harder to understand the client and their needs" than any other firm. This resulted in the evolution of a particular kind of designer and some of the smartest, most beautifully logical work (particularly annual reports) ever created.

48

Strategists or planners can be designers' best friends, especially if they provide meaningful consumer insights and help the designer to navigate and process the client's culture—particularly if that client consists of a number of different stakeholders with varying points of view. A planner can even help the designer arrive at a beautifully logical solution, as a sounding board and with periodic reality checks. A planner can help get the client to buy into the designer's approach. And help keep the client on strategy. And help sell through otherwise challenging work. In fact, this is where a planner can become a designer's very best friend.

All of this involves creating a logical system, a new and (hopefully) improved creative process. But the designers have to be the ones driving it, or I fear that these extremely well-meaning and adventurous design and hybrid firms will end up being nothing more than glorified production artists—or worse, advertising agencies.

~~MORE OF YOU AND LESS OF THEM IS BEST FOR THEM~~

3.0 MIN.

To me, the term "applied art" is all about math. It's all about math because the two words represent such different concepts that it's almost an oxymoron. Despite the fact that even what we refer to as "fine art" is, at some level, applied, by virtue of the fact that collectors and museums buy it and people pay to see it, we have "target audiences," and the fact that "premium brand name" artists like Damien Hirst can sell a diamond-encrusted skull for just shy of $200 million makes it hard not to bandy about terms like "brand equity" and "the art market."

Then, there's the architecture question: is anyone really prepared to say that Antoni Gaudí or Frank Lloyd Wright or Rem Koolhaas are not artists of the highest order who can comfortably take their rightful places in history alongside Picasso and Warhol and Hirst? Does MoMA's permanent collection of architectural drawings and models make it any less of an art museum? Those rhetorical questions asked, I will tell you that I view architecture as the poster child for the applied arts—complete with clients, briefs, budgets, and deliverables.

Just like graphic design.

Which leads me to my topic. Generally, we distinguish between fine art and applied art by saying that fine art is fundamentally about the inspiration and vision of the artist, while applied art is about the inspiration and vision of the artist in the service of a paying client. All talk of "art markets" aside, let's use these distinctions to explore this fascinating bit of math that affects you and me (and our work and client dynamics) on every project we touch, whether we're aware of it at the time or not.

Pies always seem to help me. Not eating them, but visualizing them. If a pie represents 100 percent of a particular piece of communication, how much of that pie should be the client's voice, and how much should be the creator's voice (or creators' voices, if a designer and a writer are working in tandem [as they should])? I know some contrarian designers who would say, "100 percent client, 0 percent creators." To them, I simply say, "Yeah, well, whatever." Many would venture, "50/50." I actually asked a bunch of people this week, and I had a surprising number of responses putting the ideal mixture at "25 percent client, 75 percent creators." I am working with a couple of my favorite designers right now on what is essentially a brand launch. The client has no established voice, no brand personality, no graphics standards manual to adhere to; we've been tasked with creating all of that. So, in this and other start-up scenarios, the ratio might be more like "10 percent client, 90 percent creators." And that is as it should be—for their sake, not just ours. (Plus, these kinds of projects are always going to be more satisfying than making little incremental tweaks to, say, Coca-Cola's rigid identity system.)

I'm not sure what the "right" mixture is, or even if that mixture would be right for every client or every project, but here's what I believe: that this poor world is bombarded with so much crap, so much literal, ham-fisted, predictable crap, every day, and that this crap eventually starts to flow together into one giant sea of crap. The Crap Sea, let's call it. The more of the voice pie we can own as creators without entirely losing our clients' message in the equation, the more powerful and memorable their messages will ultimately be, and the more money they will make, and the more freedom they will give us to explore and experiment and do what fulfills us most: applying our art.

52

DESIGNERS VERSUS ADVERTISING ART DIRECTORS

4.0 MIN.

A thought has been bugging me for a while. Actually, two thoughts have been bugging me for a while.

One, how is it that so much of Paul Rand's work still holds up and resonates today?

Two, why is it that I enjoy working with graphic designers so much more than I do advertising art directors?

I think there may be one answer to both questions.

What's ironic is that for years, I listened to advertising people disparage designers as "not conceptual." Or worse, say that a designer's idea of "concept" is nothing more than type and color. And I have come across a handful of "designers" who seem bent on perpetuating that stereotype. When I tell some of my advertising friends about my decision to only work with great designers (and not art directors), I almost inevitably get a mixed reaction of befuddlement and pity, as if I have somehow relegated myself to the backwaters of the communications world. I can see it in their eyes: "Type and color."

But here's the truth: the reason I love working with great designers more than I do with even those considered to be "great" advertising art directors is that great designers are far more conceptual, strategic, logical, intellectual, and systematic in their approach to problems than the most award-winning, diva art directors I have worked with over the years. The designers that I am fortunate enough to work with make even the best art directors seem shallow and irrelevant. I've said it before, but I don't believe there are many true art directors anymore. Lots of

55

ad directors rearranging things they've seen in other ads, but not many people directing art.

I recently had the opportunity to work with one of my favorite designers on a project for a big pharmaceutical company. We were hired by the big pharmaceutical company's equally big advertising agency to develop some ideas in addition to the ones being developed by the agency. This designer has her own process, which is unlike any art director's process I've observed. I was blown away by how deeply she and her team of designers got into the brief and the research and the problem itself. There were debates, discussions, more research, countless questions (and I was counting), breakout sessions, and many late nights spent just trying to wrap our heads around the problem. The end result was amazing. Flawless logic, beautifully executed. When we saw some of the work the agency had done, the thinking (at least to me) seemed shallow and undeveloped in comparison. The other agency had had a year to work on it; we had a couple of weeks.

So, the reason I think Rand's work still resonates today, and the reason I will only work with great designers until the day I die? Check out this quote from the maestro himself:

"My interest has always been in restating the validity of those ideas which, by and large, have guided artists since the time of Polyclitus. I believe that it is only in the application of those timeless principles that one can even begin to achieve a semblance of quality in one's work. It is the continuing relevance of these ideals that I mean to emphasize, especially to those who have grown up in a world of punk and graffiti."

Somewhere, David Carson is weeping.

Just taken at face value, Rand's quote is deep enough. But if you dig a little deeper and refresh your memory about the canon of Polyclitus, you again see the difference between art directors and designers. There are cheesy statues everywhere. And then there are those who are (knowingly or unknowingly) informed by the work and teaching of Polyclitus, who revolutionized sculpture by meticulously and painstakingly bringing human emotion into the equation. Dig deeper still and you see that Polyclitus's vision of "the beautiful" and "the perfect" was influenced by Pythagoras, who believed that reality consisted of ten sets of opposites:

limited and unlimited

odd and even

one and plurality

right and left

male and female

rest and movement

straight and curved

light and darkness

good and bad

square and oblong

Rand operated out of this kind of intellectual, systematic approach to problem-solving, but always with heaping helpings of inspiration, craft, and wit. It seems to me that every great designer I have worked with also

57

operates out of this rich, intellectual, almost poetic place. It's not just type and color. I once asked one of my favorite designers why he always uses Helvetica. He told me that he spends so much time thinking about the problem that he rarely has time left over to "design" the piece. I think he was being a tad coy (he's one of the most awarded designers of the past decade), but he made his point: Designers are not decorators; they are problem solvers. And it takes brains to solve problems, not just taste.

~~ART DIRECTORS~~
~~DON'T ANYMORE~~

5.0 MIN.

Someone asked me this week, "Austin, what do you have against art directors?" It made me think of that moment in *The Fountainhead* when Ellsworth Toohey says to Howard Roark, "Why don't you tell me what you think of me," and Roark answers, "But I don't think of you."

I haven't thought of art directors since I made the decision to work solely with graphic designers. My work—and my life—has been richer for it. But I thought I'd share with you my response to the question. It might confirm some of your own suspicions about your so-called advertising counterparts.

Advertising art directors differ from graphic designers and magazine art directors in that they are primarily engaged in advertising, and advertising is more about the selling proposition than it is the holistic, concrete piece of work that communicates the selling proposition. When advertising people say, "It's all about the idea," what they generally mean is, "It's all about the selling proposition." Relatively little thought is given by the art director to the actual creative product or the various components of the creative product—typography, photography, illustration, layout, materials, etc. In that sense, advertising is much more utilitarian than design. By utilitarian, I mean that the end disregards the means. A strip mall can be useful, but it rarely meets our needs for beauty or a respectful, intelligent human experience.

Because advertising has become so utilitarian (with the occasional exception of television commercials, where agencies "add on" executionally-focused film directors), art directors—and the various schools teaching art direction—don't go very deep into "art," i.e., photography, illustration, typography, layout, printing, materials, design theory and criticism, etc. Occasionally, an advertising agency will have what appears to be a moment of self-awareness, and it will engage an award-winning design firm to "plus" its mediocre ideas, visually. Agencies don't want full immersion in the design process (which might challenge their process, if not their very existence). They prefer sprinkling. But this unnatural act of designers "decorating" agency ideas after the fact is a bit like wrapping shit in a Hermès scarf. It might look pretty, but it's still shit.

Most designers approach each assignment as an intellectual, aesthetic, holistic problem to be solved. (The client's selling proposition may be part of that equation, but it is by no means the only part.) They have (hopefully) studied art, art history, the relatively recent history of graphic design, modernism, structuralism, all the other "isms," layout, color, typography, photography and photographic techniques and trends and who the current players are, illustration and who the current players are, and so on. Hopefully, they have studied a little film, as well. Some have, depending on their education.

The net result: a project developed by an advertising art director (with a copywriter, both answering to a creative director) will typically have a "concept"—an idea that communicates some benefit or point about the advertiser, with relatively little thought given to the actual piece itself. Being utilitarian in nature (especially in the U.S.), the idea will generally be very literal at best and ham-fisted or spoon-fed at worst.

A piece of communication developed by a designer (sometimes paired with a writer, and answering to a creative director or design director) is very considered and well thought out, with every aspect of the communication given equal import. It will generally be something balanced, be beautiful to look at and possibly to touch, and may be more abstract or poetic. Because skilled designers have been trained and are aware of the "engineering" and theory behind communication itself (semiotics), they not only have a relatively encyclopedic knowledge of different font families, for instance, but they also know how and why certain fonts exist at all, and how the human mind interprets various symbols and ideas. Their talent may have submerged some of this knowledge so that it operates on a more intuitive level, but nevertheless, it's there. Not so with 98.5 percent of the art directors in this country. That number drops substantially in the U.K. and other parts of Europe, where advertising and the requisite education for advertising practitioners is far less utilitarian and involves more of a background in fine art and design theory. Two of the biggest sources of new "talent" for U.S. agencies are Portfolio Center and Creative Circus. I have taught at both. Their names hint at the pragmatism of their curricula: these schools exist to get their graduates employed, not to make them great.

Jay Chiat once said, "Art directors are a dime a dozen." I was a bit shocked when he said it, especially given that his protégé and successor, Lee Clow, is himself an art director. But I think I understand what Chiat meant. He was a serious art collector and patron of Frank Gehry before anyone knew who Frank Gehry was. I think he saw the superficiality of the art directors who worked at his agency. He could see the gap between the fine arts and his agency's work—and his agency's work was (and is) pretty good, as agency work goes.

As I have said before, I believe that the two (advertising and design) shall become one again—as they were in the beginning, but I don't think the fusion will come from the advertising agency side. Agencies have too

63

much to concede, too much to learn, and too many bad habits to break. Agencies would rather sprinkle design on their advertising than be fully immersed in a new systematic way of thinking and working. Rather, I think it will be design firms expanding their scope and vision to embrace all kinds of communication—including advertising. Some already have.

~~THE DEATH OF ADVERTISING: UNENLIGHTENED SELF-INTEREST~~

5.5 MIN.

In the chapter on creative destruction, I posit that the only truly "bad" news is "middle" news, or (temporarily) blissful ignorance. In this chapter, I have good news and middle news: the middle news is that most of the advertising industry is in a state of paralysis brought on by a stubborn resistance to change. The good news is that this presents some significant new business opportunities for my favorite design firms— if they choose to pounce on those opportunities.

A few years ago, I decided that advertising was dying. By advertising, I don't mean the ongoing dialogue between brands and their customers, because that dialogue will continue as long as there are brands and customers. But the means of engaging in that dialogue are changing rapidly and, by and large, the advertising industry is just not keeping pace. I believe there are two primary reasons for this:

1. Advertising people tend to be followers instead of leaders. The leaders stand out, and the rest of the industry stands around waiting to see what the leaders will do, or for the next short film or pop culture phenomenon to co-opt.

2. As differentiation between agencies becomes more difficult, firms become more insular and more deeply entrenched in outmoded methodologies.

Fallon in Minneapolis started out with a clear if Machiavellian business development program: do work for small, appreciative clients (hair salons, restaurants, muffler shops, etc.), dominate awards competitions, and parlay that fame into bigger, more visible accounts. It worked remarkably well. So well, in fact, that the rest of the industry followed its model. And it worked again (Chiat). And again (Goodby).

67

And *again* (Crispin), to the point where winning awards became the raison d'être—the cake, and not merely the icing.

Adrian Shaughnessy says, "It is well known in advertising that winning industry awards is sometimes the primary concern of an agency's creative staff, and because of this, clients often accuse agencies of ignoring their needs in favor of creating work that appeals to judges who sit on awards panels (usually fellow practitioners)."

Some clients play along; after all, who *doesn't* want a free trip to Cannes or Miami and the prestige that comes with being an award-winning client? But honestly, I'm just not sure that the things juries are looking for are necessarily the same things that consumers are looking for in the brand-customer dialogue.

I do think certain creative competitions contribute, on some level, to the craft of advertising and design. And I can buy the argument that a piece of communication that grabs the attention of a jaded juror is also likely to grab the attention of an advertising-sated consumer. But I can't shake the feeling that advertising people are just talking to themselves—and increasingly so.

One could also argue that it's the duty of every creative person to know what else is being done out there and that award annuals and trade magazines can provide a snapshot. But there are things going on in the broader creative community of the fine arts, architecture, fashion, music, and industrial design that provide far more inspiration than what advertising creative directors thought was good last year.

The ability to craft arresting communication should be a given for any practicing professional. Innovation doesn't come from studying what other people are doing in your space, but from trying new things, creating new connections, and cross-pollinating between disciplines.

If I was appointed worldwide creative director of all advertising agencies for a day (admittedly a scary thought for all involved), I would make one major, sweeping change: I would put a moratorium on all advertising award shows and trade publications (including *Archive* and *Adweek*). If an agency did a remarkable television or radio commercial, I would encourage it to enter it in Cannes (I know that Cannes's radio category is still in its infancy, but theoretically, Cannes could become the elite creative show for all broadcast). If the agency did something remarkable in print or design or even digital, I would let it enter it in D&AD (you generally have to do something extraordinary to get past the tough and occasionally provincial British judges). The Effies would be legal. Submitting work to more credible creative publications like *ID*, *Graphis*, and *Eye* would also be permissible. But I would—for an indefinite period of time—withdraw from entering all local and regional competitions, as well as CA Advertising and Design, One Show Advertising and Design, Type Directors Club, Art Directors Club, the CLIOs, the ANDYs, London International Awards, and all of the other competitions. Nothing would prevent clients from entering work in their industry-specific competitions (which they seem to cherish more than pencils and other, more "prestigious" awards).

Instead of trade pubs, I would use the millions of dollars in savings derived from cutting award show entry budgets to have every agency subscribe to *ID*, *Graphis*, *Eye*, *Nylon*, *Tank*, *Dwell*, *Wallpaper*, *Surface*,

W, MD, and any other architecture, interior design, fashion, photography, or art magazine that features the most interesting work being done globally. I would use some of the savings to have interesting people from all walks of life (politicians, futurists, economists, furniture designers, hoteliers, physicists, etc.) come in and conduct salon-like dialogues with the entire staff on a broad range of topics. I would also build libraries of the most interesting new bands, artists, and architects in each agency.

Some firms have already started moving in this direction, most notably Wieden+Kennedy and JDK. Their work and their cultures reflect the added interest of embracing the larger creative community.

Finally, a prediction: clients are tiring of agency self-interest. They know. Many of them have done time on the agency side and know what drives many of the better-known firms. If the advertising industry does not wake up to its potential role in the entire brand experience that a customer has with its clients' companies, those clients will begin to revolt. They will leave their award-winning firms for *customer*-winning firms—ones that take a more holistic approach to the ongoing brand-customer dialogue and get involved in everything from product design to the retail environment to the brand's approach to corporate responsibility to the customers' satisfaction long after they've purchased their clients' products.

This may, in fact, be the best time in recent history for design firms with these capabilities to approach desirable brands. But, as the car ads say: "This opportunity won't last, so you'd better hurry!" It is possible that advertising agencies will see the light—especially when their award-winning clients start jumping ship and hiring my favorite designers.

70

DESIGN REQUIRES FULL IMMERSION, NOT SPRINKLING OR POURING

6.0 MIN.

One of the silly, divisive doctrines that Catholics and Protestants often debate is the practice of baptism. The Catholic tradition is to ceremoniously sprinkle a little holy water on infants, while the Protestants insist that it must be full immersion (for adolescents and adults)—or nothing. For the sake of this essay, I will take the Protestant position, only because I have become convinced that advertising agencies, by and large, have embraced a kind of magical thinking that by just sprinkling or pouring some design onto their advertising, it will be saved from being boring, derivative, and uninspired. They feel even holier when they go to the extent of adding a design department to their agencies, which might be the equivalent of pouring as opposed to merely sprinkling. This may help the agency turn out better collateral, but my experience has been that unless the advertising agency embarks on a wholesale, fundamental change at a cellular level to embrace design—as a system, as a way of thinking, as almost a lifestyle—design will always be thought of as an add-on, something to be applied to their ads. Sprinkled. Poured. There's even a term for it (which makes me a little nauseous): "sweetening." An advertising agency subcontracts with a design firm to "sweeten" their ads. This is fine, if by "sweetening" they mean "tackle the marketing problem and approaching it logically, holistically, thoroughly." But I have been on the design side of these sweetening efforts, and even if the design firm is successful at creating a far more sweeping, elegant, powerful solution than the agency's, politics and professional pride seldom allow the agency to champion the designers' work with their clients. The outcome is often, "We love what you've done; it's perfect really, but we just want you to make our ideas look better." Design as decoration. Sprinkling.

In theory, Anomaly (in New York) and Taxi (in Toronto and New York) have made attempts at immersion and talk the hybrid talk: Anomaly added an advertising creative director to what was essentially a design practice, and Taxi intermingled design and advertising vis-à-vis the company's partnership structure. I say "in theory" because, to be honest, I haven't seen the fruits of full immersion yet from either of these two agencies. Wieden+Kennedy has folded in serious designers like John Jay and Todd Waterbury to their already creative milieu, but despite these designers' credentials and influence (all positive), Wieden still remains largely a traditional advertising agency, albeit one of the most creative in the world. Still, when you think of Wieden, you think of epic television commercials for the most part, not of design or hybrid.

Where I look first to observe the hybrid model's progress is JDK in Vermont, where the lines between design and branding and communications and advertising and even product design are all being blurred. I look to Sandstrom Partners in Portland, whose DNA contains collaborations with traditional agencies. It is often tasked with creating ad campaigns for their design clients. I look to Cahan & Associates in San Francisco, which parlayed its fame as the most creative annual report firm in the world to become a sophisticated communications company and recently took on global advertising duties for the Aldo brand. Then, there is a handful of other, smaller firms that are smart enough and flexible enough to invite immersion: Opolis, Cinco, Nemo, Bob Dinetz, Fredrik Averin, even Razorfish (not small, but somehow agile enough to occasionally immerse itself in both digital and traditional advertising modes).

I see it more clearly and more profoundly every day:

The advertising world is over here.

And the design world is over here.

The two must fuse, and if you press the top practitioners from both worlds, they will tell you as much. But it must be fusion and not addition—or even collaboration (although that wouldn't be a bad start). And this is where things so often get stuck, because nobody is willing to completely cede to the other: the advertising people think that designers are all about color stories and typefaces and fancy borders—that designers don't "get" concepts or ideas. The designers think that advertising people are tasteless, superficial cretins whose idea of a concept is a snappy headline and an ironic visual. Catholics versus Protestants, I'm afraid. From where I sit, I don't see the creative fusion that will take us back to the power and effectiveness of the original Doyle Dane Bernbach advertising or the work of Paul Rand or William Golden coming from the advertising side. There's too much to give up, especially given that agencies are typically retained by their clients on an ongoing basis, while design firms typically (but not always) are engaged for specific projects from clients with no promise of future work. The design world has less to lose and more to gain. Here's a whole world of (advertising) content that is ugly, derivative, and illogical, and just begging for a smart, strategic design firm to grab onto it and shape it. And that's the key: agencies are not capable of great design, but design firms are capable of great advertising. Most of them don't have the media planning or buying expertise, but guess what? More and more clients are unbundling their media and handing it off to media experts while paying their agencies

75

a fee for creative services. So, there's never been a better time for design firms to cross over and start owning all manner of a client's branded communications, i.e., print, outdoor, television, and even radio. (I've spoken before about the similarities between audio and design.) It's all open. And I haven't even touched on the digital world.

Recently, I had a conversation with the creative director of a highly regarded, award-winning advertising agency. He mentioned that his agency was looking to hire a senior designer and asked me for some recommendations. When I probed a bit more about the position and asked if the agency was ready to rethink its creative approach to fully integrate design into the agency process, he laughed and said, "Are you kidding me? Our owners would never go for that. We just need someone to do collateral and logos and shit." I didn't mention any of your names at that point. I repeat: highly regarded, award-winning advertising agency. This is why I don't hold out much hope that a great fusion that'll marshal all of the skills and disciplines from both industries to form one concentrated powerhouse of branded communication will come from advertisingland. Hell, even Wieden—with John freakin' Jay—can't get it done. But keep your eyes on the design practices I mentioned above. One by one, clients will start to see the value and holistic capabilities of design firms relative to advertising agencies. And the design firm that's doing Keen Footwear's advertising will soon be doing ESPN's advertising. The design firm responsible for Aldo's global advertising duties will soon get a call to work on a major automobile's advertising. The designers doing ads for Kettle Chips will be asked to do a Super Bowl commercial for a beer brand. And so on, until the big advertising holding companies meet in one of their fancy locales to discuss the state of the advertising business and decide that there's only one thing they can do to stop this mass exodus of clients defecting to graphic design firms for all of their branded communications:

"We must hire designers. To do collateral and logos and shit."

~~MAYBE YOU'D DO BETTER WORK IF YOU WENT IN-HOUSE~~

6.0 MIN.

There is another "Golden" age of design right around this next turn.

I just procured a wonderful bit of '60s ephemera. (If you live within meeting distance from me, you've no doubt already seen it.) It's called *The Visual Craft of William Golden*, and it is about a man who has become one of my heroes in recent years for one primary reason.

He almost single-handedly commandeered an entire corporation's (CBS) communications and fought hard, well, and consistently to make every piece of communication that went out from that company a gift to the intended audience. And he did this for an entire decade. By "gift," I mean:

More intelligent than it probably needed to be. Every piece showed a respect for the intended audience's intellect.

Pared down and edited to only the most essential information. (If you've done work for any of the networks, you know that this was no small task.)

Demonstrated a respect for the intended audience's time.

Every ad, every promotional piece, and every corporate design piece was of a consistently high aesthetic quality. He was able to talk his bosses into using the best illustrators, photographers, and other suppliers. This shows a respect for the intended audience's sense of aesthetics.

All of his stuff, though sophisticated, seemed also to have an element of playfulness to it—the kind of playfulness that betrays a passionate commitment to the category and to some kind of vision. It was like Apple: you can't be that flip and offhanded about your competitive position against PCs without a deep, 24/7, win-at-any-cost, ruthless seriousness

79

about unseating that foe. Like the axiom "you have to know the rules to break them," maybe it's true that "you have to be serious about what you're doing in order to not be."

Check out just a few pages of the William Golden portfolio, which spanned a decade with an impossible consistency and an even more impossible freshness. It's not that there aren't designers that are capable of this today, but the execs at the networks don't have the gravitas to stick with anything. Right?

Okay, here's my thought:

Maybe you should go in-house and rid the world of bad design and advertising for the next ten to twenty years.

By "go in-house," I don't mean that anyone needs to leave their current firm. But maybe you should look for clients—first on your existing roster— whom you could infiltrate (even more), whose political landscape you have learned to navigate, who will listen to you, and who can be convinced to become patrons of ten years of gifts to their audience. Paul Rand was ostensibly the in-house designer for several of his clients, most notably IBM. JDK might as well be the in-house design department for Burton; Fredrik Averin might as well have been the in-house graphic design department for Seagate; and so on. These firms are deep inside of their respective clients' businesses, and it shows. It shows in every tiny detail that goes out from those two brands. I collect collateral I love, and part of that collection is a tiny, round piece of printed matter that came with my last Burton jacket. It was just a funny line drawing showing you how to zip or unzip the hat. The obviousness of that little gift elicits a smile every time. Seagate's FreeAgent Go portable drive packaging

80

has a top that opens up like the petals of a flower, with the words, "It loves me," "It loves me not," and "It loves me and wants to go everywhere I go" on each "petal" as you open it, and a quick start guide with approximate times (displayed on an illustrated clock in the corner) it should take to set up the drive so you can see how you compare to the average.

I hope these guys don't give up. I hope JDK never becomes so top-of-the-line that below-the-line is no longer sacred ground to it. I hope Averin doesn't grow weary of small-minded client push-back or push-back from the dreaded "field." I hope that Wieden never becomes so big and "strategic" that it stops bringing unexpected little gifts that don't appear anywhere in the brief to Nike. Besides, if they do stop, some ambitious junior team at Crispin will start.

I hope that my favorite designers ultimately take over the entire corporate universe, do away with everything that is stupid, irrelevant, and aesthetically toxic, and replace it with beautiful logic. If they could (and I am so willing to help), and build even just ten years of momentum, like Golden did, the impact of that would be felt—and seen—well beyond our lifetimes.

Ten years.

Golden and CBS. Rand and IBM. DDB and VW. Arnold and VW. Wieden and Nike. Chiat and Apple. JDK and Burton. Sandstrom and Tazo. This is rarefied air.

You know all those Bullshit™ proprietary processes that advertising and design firms dream up to differentiate themselves? The best one I've heard about requires that clients pay a ridiculous amount of money over several days during a pitch to basically share all of their sensitive branding and marketing issues in a context that places the agency in the role of "expert" and almost guarantees that it wins the business. And if it doesn't, hey, it just got paid a boatload of cash to learn the category.

Maybe one of us should launch a new branded design process called Deca-Brand™ or some variation on that theme that requires the prospective client to commit to a ten-year engagement to make sure that every touchpoint with the consumer is impacted in a meaningful way, with enough momentum (and enough teeth built into the contract) to basically ensure another decade or more of brand equity. (Dequity™?)

Or, should we just initiate today a personal and companywide ten-year commitment to make everything we do for every client into a gift? We could marshal all of our wits, wisdom, experience, creativity, and negotiating skills to basically commandeer the communications programs of each of our clients and do what Golden did.

One of my favorite designers was telling me that she went and heard Paul Rand speak before he died. She said, "He was old and crotchety. I got the feeling he was thinking, 'Screw 'em!' most of the time. Funny stories, though. Seems like good designers are all control freaks, battling the forces of ugly." I would only add that good designers are control freaks battling the forces of ugly *and illogical.*

I am 100 percent pro-control-freak-designers-battling-the-forces-of-ugly-and-illogical.

Please be encouraged in the midst of your current battle, be it ever so calm and collaborative. Maybe you should think about this: ten years from now, an anthology will be published of all of your work for your current client(s). Ads, Web pages, annual reports, hangtags, bill stuffers, exhibits—everything. And it all looks as consistent and fresh as Golden's.

HOW MANY IDEAS SHOULD YOU PRESENT?

2.0 MIN.

A few days ago, I was speaking with one of my favorite designers and a certain advertising creative director about what we should show to a client—specifically, how much of our thinking we should bring forward in our next meeting with them. The creative director was arguing for more (something about "creative due diligence"), and the designer and I were lobbying for less (something about "having a point of view"). When we reached an impasse in the conversation, I asked if I could read something that I had stumbled across that morning. They humored me. What I read to them was from *A Designer's Art* by Paul Rand, and it broke the deadlock. The advertising creative director asked, "Where the hell did that come from?" I explained that it came from a designer.

You may have read this before, but even if you have, I will get as much out of reprinting it here as you will out of reading it again. It might even alter what—and how much—you present to your clients this week.

One of the more common problems, which tends to create doubt and confusion, is caused by the inexperienced and anxious executive who innocently expects, or even demands, to see not one but many solutions to a problem. These may include a number of visual and verbal concepts, an assortment of layouts, a variety of pictures and color schemes, as well as a choice of type styles. He needs the reassurance of numbers and the opportunity to exercise his personal preferences. He is also most likely to be the one to insist on endless revisions with unrealistic deadlines, adding to an already wasteful and time-consuming ritual. Theoretically, a great number of ideas assures a great number of choices, but such choices are essentially quantitative. This practice is as bewildering as it is wasteful. It discourages spontaneity, encourages indifference, and more often than not, produces results that are neither distinguished, interesting, nor effective. In short, good ideas rarely come in bunches.

He then turns to advertising people:

Advertising agencies can be especially guilty in this numbers game. Bent on impressing the client with their ardor, they present a welter of layouts, many of which are superficial interpretations of potentially good ideas or slick renderings of trite ones.

The bottom line, Rand posits, is a lack of confidence and courage:

The designer who voluntarily presents his client with a batch of layouts does so not out of prolificacy, but out of uncertainty or fear. He thus encourages the client to assume the role of referee… Expertise in business administration, journalism, accounting, or selling, though necessary in its place, is not expertise in problems dealing with visual appearance.

Testicular strength. That's what we need.

THE POWER OF CURIOSITY AND CAMARADERIE TO GET YOU OUT OF A CREATIVE RUT

2.0 MIN.

In 1912, the Salon des Indépendants in Paris attracted a rather unusual group of conventioneers. Those ubiquitous red and white adhesive name badges would have read, "HELLO, MY NAME IS…" Pablo Picasso, Juan Gris, Piet Mondrian, or Diego Rivera. Quite an interesting bunch to run into in the hotel's piano bar in the wee hours.

The Mexican artist Rivera brought an odd little artifact with him to Paris: a two thousand-year-old head that had three eyes and two mouths so that a full face could be seen at the same time as a profile from nearly any angle. He shared his little gem with Picasso, who was quite taken with the piece. So taken, in fact, that it informed nearly his every portrait of man and beast from that point forward until his death in 1973. Whenever you see a woman or man or bull or horse in Picasso's post-1912 work, you can see the effect that Rivera's show-and-tell had on his oeuvre. His technique of showing the same subject from several different angles simultaneously was foreshadowed in my all-time favorite, *Les Demoiselles d'Avignon*, which is often pointed to as the advent of cubism. But no doubt this sculpture helped to cement his unique, unprecedented vision. (It's interesting to note that Rivera never really availed himself of the cubist lessons his artifact provided for his Spanish colleague.)

I have a few favorite designers whom I would classify as "enthusiasts." By that, I mean that when we get together, we are always apt to share our latest "finds" or treasures scoured from Powell's or eBay or Abe Books. I actually have what amounts to a shrine of *objets d'art* in my basement, the most cherished of which end up in my office as inspiration. Some of those objects were probably designed by you; others, I have scavenged from the global design repository. On occasion, the consequence of my

89

camaraderie with these enthusiasts and the curiosity we share is a new direction for my work, or a new direction for theirs. My writing has been inspired on more than one occasion by artifacts shared back and forth among friends. It's something I encourage you to try within your studio or among you and your colleagues. You never know—as Rivera couldn't have known—the kind of impact that one little discovery can have.

CREATIVE DESTRUCTION AND THE FUTURE ADVANTAGES OF MEDIOCRITY

3.0 MIN.

So, there was this Harvard economist in the '40s with the unfortunate name of Joseph Schumpeter. He had this idea he called "creative destruction," about "the tendency of a free market economy to incessantly revitalize itself from within by scrapping old and failing businesses and then reallocating resources to newer, more productive ones." I.e., the Pony Express was displaced by newer, more productive telegraph technology, which was displaced by newer, more productive telephone technology, which is now being displaced by newer, more productive computer and wireless technology, and (eventually) so on.

But I think this whole progress and obsolescence thing might apply to individuals, design firms, ad agencies, and specific industries as much as it does to a country's economy. And the implication is that there is good news, middle news, and no truly "bad" news—except for the middle news. (Stay with me for three more paragraphs, and I promise that this sentence will make sense.)

There is good news for strong brand leaders, the "newer, more productive" businesses. The ones that are not just strong numerically but creatively and internally, as well. They will continue to grow and become stronger, providing they keep their collective eye on the ball. According to Schumpeter's creative destruction theory, the economy (or design firm or ad agency) that finds itself at a severe disadvantage is potentially in a very good place, as well, because it's well positioned for (and probably highly motivated toward) revitalization.

It's the firms in the middle, the ones that are just chugging along, making a decent living doing decent work (not bad, not great), that, if there is any weight to the creative destruction theory, are in the most precarious and scary place. They're just not aware of it yet. In other words: ignorance is bliss, until—suddenly—it isn't anymore.

One "newer, more productive" firm, Wieden+Kennedy, revitalized itself and the entire advertising space by "reallocating resources" like John Jay and Todd Waterbury. However, I sometimes forget that this strong brand leader started out in a basement with a card table and a pay phone at the end of the hall. Crispin Porter+Bogusky started out with the perceived disadvantage of being located in Florida. Legend has it that Alex Bogusky was once turned down for a creative job at W+K, which fueled his fervor to turn CP+B into "the next Wieden+Kennedy." Believable, since disadvantage seems to propel people to achieve things they might not have otherwise achieved.

One of the most awarded and influential designers in America likes to remind people that "some of the world's largest corporations have entrusted their image to a guy who spent much of his formative youth living in a trailer court in Clackamas, Oregon."

The most recent example of creative destruction and the future advantages of mediocrity is a firm that I will simply refer to as "A." It first showed up on my radar several years and name changes ago. I perceived it to be one of those mediocre advertising-slash-marketing firms back when "marketing" simply meant "money grubbing." As you'll soon see, it must have had some smart and talented people hidden in the building somewhere, but in terms of its creative product and reputation, it was bad news. After endless mergers and acquisitions (honestly, I lost track), the firm changed its name a few more times just for fun, and somehow came out so far ahead of the curve that it kind of makes my head spin. Suddenly, that "old and failing" advertising-slash-marketing firm is one of the most sophisticated interactive design firms in the country.

Like most writers, I always feel the need to wrap up my endings with a neat little logic bow. But I'm going to leave the conclusion here to you, in case you even want a conclusion. It could maybe start with something like, "Okay, so if you're a strong brand leader…"

CAREER LAUNCHERS

2.0 MIN.

One of my favorite designers turned me on to Alexey Brodovitch, the Russian émigré who basically revolutionized magazine design in the '30s, '40s, and '50s, while he was art director at *Harper's Bazaar* (among other things). I knew his name and reputation; it's almost impossible to read anything about graphic design within the past century without his name coming up. But I didn't realize what an amazing visionary and creative leader he was, or what an impact he had on visual communication in this country.

As I read about Brodovitch, I couldn't help thinking about people like Michael Jager, Bill Cahan, Susan Hoffman, and Steve Sandstrom— people who have launched the careers of so many creative people, not just art directors and designers and copywriters, but photographers, illustrators, filmmakers, and other artists who have gone on to do great things. I have run into so many people who credit Jager with "giving them their start" that a few of us have begun to joke about him being "the Kevin Bacon of design." Six degrees of Michael Jager.

I think a lot of times it's born of necessity—necessity being the mother of invention. You don't have a Tony Scott or a Richard Burbridge budget, so you search for the hungry, up-and-coming star and you give them some freedom, and suddenly, you have a famous piece of creative work and a famous director or photographer in the bargain.

Brodovitch used to take yearly sojourns to Europe to uncover new creative talent, much like Hoffman used to take weekly sojourns to Rich's Cigar Store (a Portland shop with an impressively well-stocked periodicals section) to look at European fashion magazines for inspiration (before that was particularly fashionable).

97

The roster of talent that Brodovitch nurtured and turned loose on the pages of *Bazaar* reads like a who's who of art and design: Jean Cocteau, Marc Chagall, A.M. Cassandre, Man Ray, and Richard Avedon, to name a few. Ray and Avedon both owe their success in the United States largely to the encouragement, support, and opportunities provided by the cranky Russian. He had ridiculously high expectations, which pushed people to exceed them.

Brodovitch reminds me that there are gems out there just waiting to be discovered, nurtured, and launched. One thing that was said of Brodovitch was that no matter how busy he was, he always made time to view photographers' portfolios, with the idea that one of them might just be the next Richard Avedon. He also gave his students at the Design Lab a lot of creative opportunities that he could have taken for himself.

I think that might have been Brodovitch's secret. (But it's not a secret anymore, because I just told you.)

~~BE INCONSISTENT FOR A CHANGE~~

2.0 MIN.

Whenever I need to be challenged or inspired or reassured that greatness is possible in the context of nervous, nearsighted clients and the
so-called practical realities of business, two things never fail me. If I'm in
Los Angeles, I will go walk around the Hollyhock House or sit in my car
and just stare at the Ennis-Brown House. If I'm in Portland, I'll flip through
a few different books that give me a survey of all of Frank Lloyd Wright's
work. I did that this week. Reviewing his Prairie House period to
Fallingwater to the textile blockhouses in California to the Johnson
Wax headquarters to the Usonian houses (one of which is in Oregon)
to the Guggenheim (my personal favorite), I was struck again by how
many unique voices Wright worked in, and how pronounced and original
each one was. I think we refer to these very different clusters of projects
as being representative of a certain "period" or "style" because each one
demonstrates such intense conviction, as if Wright believed that each
building preempted all others before and after it. Time has pretty much
vindicated that belief. Although there is a thread of organic architecture
throughout all of his work and an almost undeniable spiritual aspect to
it, the buildings from period to period look and feel so radically different.
It's almost as if Wright lived at least five and as many as ten different lives
and came back as an incredibly talented and visionary architect each
time—but each time with an entirely different vision. It reminded me of
one of my favorite quotes, by Ralph Waldo Emerson in *Self-Reliance*:

"A foolish consistency is the hobgoblin of little minds."

I always considered Winston Churchill to be the poster child for that
principle, flip-flopping back and forth from party to party, from policy to
policy, but always with deep and admirable conviction and an openness
to change. "Deep and admirable conviction and an openness to

101

change." I think that pretty much describes Wright—and every single creative person I respect.

In *Eating the Big Fish*, Adam Morgan lists "Break With Your Immediate Past" as the first credo for challenger brands. He cites companies that have done that and have subsequently been able to see the real opportunities for radical growth and get innovative ideas by gaining a new and vital innocence.

Change things up. Do something new. Start over. Consistency is overrated.

Just ask Frank Lloyd Wright.

OCD AND MODERNISM

0.5 MIN.

The poet W.H. Auden was either a tad OCD or just an extremely passionate person.

In his musings on modernism in the 1930s, he wrote:

Clear from the head the masses of impressive rubbish

Make action urgent and its nature clear

Look shining at / New styles of architecture, a change of heart

"A well-stated problem is more than half solved… A designer transforms constraint into opportunity."

— *Viktor Frankl*

105

~~WRITERS SHOULD DRAW AND DESIGNERS SHOULD WRITE~~

2.0 MIN.

After reading a provocative essay by James McMullan on the lost art of drawing, I decided that I would spend at least half an hour every night drawing in my journal. (Right now, I'm particularly good at horses, cars, and boobies.) My hypothesis: it's not about *drawing* better, it's about *seeing* better, or seeing more and seeing more accurately. My hope: that it will make me a better, more precise communicator. McMullan says, "Drawing brings into balance the literary and graphic aspects of our design. When we draw well, we can use it as a kind of alchemical process to distill word ideas and image ideas down to whatever really works between them." Going back through my concept journals from the past three years, I'm struck by the ratio of (rough) drawings and images to words.

On the flip side, I think designers make good writers. You probably won't meet designers who think they can write that well—except for maybe Steven Heller. But I have secretly and repeatedly tested this theory, and I have become convinced of its validity. It actually makes perfect sense when you think about it: designers spend their lives organizing and ordering information in order to deliver that information in the most compelling, memorable, and pleasing way possible. The best designers are not decorators but editors, removing everything that is nonessential. Writers, on the other hand, feel the need to supply words that will ultimately convey ideas or stories of some kind, often losing objectivity and the ability to edit in the process. They become *word generators*. A good designer knows how to wade through the words, find the pure essence of an idea, and convey that idea or tell that story in as few words as possible.

And now, a confession: I have actually hired graphic designers to edit my writing on certain projects. And not only have I hired graphic designers to edit my writing, I have studied their edits to learn how they process pieces and why they make certain changes. There is a compression and an intelligence to a designer's writing that makes it feel more interesting, more respectful of the reader.

That's my goal when I write: conciseness, interest, respect for the reader. I want to write like designers would write—if they could write.

108

~~SOMETIMES THE MOST INSPIRING THING YOU CAN SAY IS NOTHING~~

0.5 MIN.

Lorem ipsum dolor sit amet consectetuer adipiscing elit lorem ipsum dolor sit amet consectetuer adipiscing elit lorem ipsum dolor sit amet consectetuer adipiscing elit lorem ipsum dolor sit amet consectetuer adipiscing elit lorem ipsum dolor sit amet consectetuer adipiscing elit lorem ipsum dolor sit amet consectetuer adipiscing elit lorem ipsum dolor sit amet consectetuer adipiscing elit lorem ipsum dolor sit amet consectetuer adipiscing elit lorem ipsum dolor sit elit lorem ipsum dolor sit amet consectetuer adipiscing elit lorem ipsum dolor sit amet consectetuer adipiscing elit lorem ipsum dolor sit amet.

Lorem ipsum dolor sit amet consectetuer adipiscing elit lorem ipsum dolor sit amet consectetuer adipiscing elit lorem ipsum dolor sit amet consectetuer adipiscing elit lorem ipsum dolor sit amet consectetuer adipiscing elit lorem ipsum dolor sit amet consectetuer adipiscing elit lorem ipsum dolor sit amet elit lorem ipsum dolor amet consectetuer.

Lorem ipsum dolor sit amet consectetuer adipiscing elit lorem ipsum dolor sit amet consectetuer adipiscing elit lorem ipsum dolor sit amet consectetuer adipiscing elit lorem ipsum dolor sit amet consectetuer adipiscing elit lorem ipsum dolor sit amet consectetuer adipiscing elit lorem ipsum dolor sit amet elit dolor sit amet consectetuer.

Lorem ipsum dolor sit amet consectetuer adipiscing elit—lorem ipsum dolor sit amet consectetuer adipiscing elit—lorem ipsum dolor sit amet consectetuer adipiscing elit lorem ipsum dolor sit amet consectetuer adipiscing elit. Lorem ipsum dolor sit amet consectetuer adipiscing elit lorem ipsum dolor sit amet consectetuer adipiscing elit lorem ipsum dolor sit amet consectetuer adipiscing *elit* lorem ipsum dolor sit amet consectetuer adipiscing elit lorem ipsum dolor sit amet… consectetuer.

OVERCOMMITMENT

3.5 MIN.

Do you know the story of Robert Garret, the track and field athlete from Baltimore? He was determined to compete in the discus throw during the 1896 Olympics in Athens, but there were two problems: one, he had never actually thrown a discus before; and two, he didn't have one to practice with. So, he asked a local blacksmith to make him a discus based on a drawing he had. It was regulation size, made of metal, and weighed about thirty pounds. After marking off the distance of the existing world record in the discus throw, Garret threw everything he had (literally) into trying to beat the record, over and over and over again, with dismal results. As the Olympics drew near, he became discouraged and finally gave up on that event—until he arrived in Athens and learned that the actual discus was made up of metal and wood, and weighed less than five pounds. He decided to compete, and even with his clumsy, comical lack of form, Garret beat the world record by nineteen centimeters.

I love this story because it reminds me that incremental efforts result in exponential change. Or, as Adam Morgan would put it, "successful brands don't commit; they *over*commit." They aim not at the surface, but two feet below the brick.

Examples of overcommitment don't exactly abound in American business, but they are out there. I recently sent a letter to Crate and Barrel thanking the company for the thoughtful and elegant design of its new retail store in Bridgeport Village, in the otherwise strip mall, big-box-store ghetto of Tualatin, Oregon. Crate and Barrel could have gotten away with a much cheaper building—its specialness is probably lost on a large percentage of people who shop there. But the company overcommitted and earned even more intense customer loyalty from at least one consumer (me).

Crate and Barrel has been overcommitting for years with its identity, its catalogues, its bags and boxes and tags. Oh, and with some of its products, too.

When Lexus, a brand "experiment" built almost entirely on over-commitment, was faced with a potentially devastating recall of eight thousand new LS400 cars, the company realized that this was an opportunity to outperform every other luxury car company in one more area. So, Lexus had its dealers drive to customers' homes or offices and pick up their cars, or had technicians go and perform the job right there—throwing in a tank of gas and a rental car. Three years later, the industry press measured all other luxury car recalls against the standard set by Lexus.

One final example—a small but personal one: I was in Los Angeles for some production and decided to stay at Shutters on the Beach in Santa Monica. As I was checking in, the fellow at the front desk handed me a fax and said, "This came for you, Mr. Howie." I smiled and corrected him, "It's actually 'Howe.'" He apologized, stopped and thought for a moment, and then informed me that he was going to upgrade me to a suite with an ocean view. Totally unnecessary, totally overcommitted, and totally appreciated. I wrote a letter to Shutters' management letting them know of this employee's awesome customer service and thanking them for their overcommitment to customer satisfaction. A week later, I received a thank-you letter for my thank-you letter. I have long believed that hotels are the last bastions of potentially perfect service in this country, and that the true test of a hotel's greatness is how it handles its "mistakes." Those moments are opportunities to create intensely loyal customers.

I'm not sure what overcommitment looks like at your firm, or in your job. But I know where it starts: with ambition and vision. And I think I know where it ends: in greatness. How many truly great design firms are there in the world right now? I think there are some, and I think there could be more if we all decided to overcommit to making history, to being great—to practicing with a thirty-pound discus.

NOCTURNAL GENIUS

3.5 MIN.

I think you might be more creative at night.

Seriously.

After years of experiencing the most vivid Technicolor dreams, I finally decided to investigate what causes them. I wasn't interested in the mystical aspects of dream interpretation, but more in whatever discoveries have been made within the neurobiological research community—that's where I hoped to find my answer. So, I started reading about Sigmund Freud's theories, Alfred Maury's experiments, Hervey de Saint-Denis and his dream journals, the more recent studies around REM (rapid eye movement) sleep, and the activation-synthesis theory of J. Allan Hobson. More important, I started paying a little more attention to my own dreams. Here's what I've concluded so far.

In the chapter "Finding Your Voice," I talk about being comfortable with your unique, distinguishable voice. I can tell you without fear of contradiction that you are never more you than when you dream. That is, you are 100 percent unedited self. So, as you fine-tune your voice as a designer, it might actually be helpful to gain some profoundly personal insights about who you are at the core through your dreams. At the very least, it's good entertainment value.

Freud believed that dreams were your brain's effort to reprocess the previous day's events. Most modern dream researchers agree with this theory. I agree with this theory. But the entertaining part of the reprocessing that goes on for about two hours every night (whether you remember your dreams or not) is the casting, art direction, and story structure of those dreams.

Dream researchers discovered as early as the late 1800s that the only way to become aware of a dream is to be awakened from it. So, they set up experiments where subjects were awakened several times throughout the night—usually during the morning hours, when REM sleep is most common. They also learned that, in most cases, the only way that people consistently remember their dreams is to write them down immediately upon waking. There is something about the type of memory employed in a sleeping state that renders even the most intense dream experience ephemeral by 11:00 A.M. if you don't write it down. The winner of the 1936 Nobel Prize, Otto Loewi, had been puzzling over an experimental problem for some time (something about the chemical transmissions of nerve impulses). One night, the answer came to him in a dream—but he didn't write it down, so he lost it. The next night, he went to bed intent on re-dreaming his crucial experiment. When he woke up, he rushed to the laboratory and came up with his Nobel Prize-winning discovery. This brings up an interesting question: can we determine what we dream? I have spoken with a number of people who share my experience of waking from a pleasant dream and then falling back to sleep and resuming that same dream.

I took it a step further to test Freud's theory that tonight's dream is a replay of today's events: as I lay in bed, I recalled the primary emotions I experienced that day and made a note of them. My dreams absolutely reflected those emotions, only through a completely different story line and with a completely different and disparate cast of characters (including a cameo by Kate Moss). Not necessarily empirical scientific evidence of any kind, but good fun, nonetheless.

So, though I have just started to delve into the subject, my conclusion thus far is this: Chances are pretty good that you will replay today's emotional events when you sleep tonight. But you will do it in an intensely creative and abstract way—not unlike good poetry, which is nonlinear and powerfully abstract. In that sense, you become a poet every night—whether you remember it or not.

My other conclusion is this: Because of the sensory restriction of sight, taste, touch (to some degree), smell, and sound (to a lesser degree) when we sleep, our other senses are more actively engaged, giving our dreams that sense of hyper-reality that makes them so powerful.

All right, even I have to admit that this is a pretty random thought. But it might add a little interest to the six to nine hours you spend with your eyes closed every night.

GRAPHIC DESIGNERS STILL HAVEN'T REALLY EMBRACED THE WEB

4.0 MIN.

Art and architectural historian Nikolaus Pevsner wrote in 1911:

"We do not reject the machine; we welcome it. But we desire to see it mastered."

One of my favorite designers said to me just the other day, "I have nothing against the Web. I just don't like having design limited by technology, and I have no desire to learn the technology." I totally understand and respect where he's coming from, but as I have been reviewing the Web sites and work of the hottest digital firms of the moment, I have come to the conclusion that, just as the worlds of design and advertising are at a critical impasse, so too are the worlds of design and interactive at the same basic full stop.

With few notable exceptions, graphic designers have so far abdicated their role in new media, perhaps for the same reason that my friend chooses to defer to "the experts." If you doubt this premise, just pay a visit to the URLs of firms like Tribal DDB, R/GA, The Barbarian Group, or Razorfish (some of the current interactive darlings here in the United States). Contrast the creativity of their work with the beautiful logic seen in the identities, packaging, environments, and collateral created by 2x4, JDK, Sandstrom Partners, Cahan & Associates, or Pentagram.

It has been estimated that there could be as many as two hundred million Web sites on the Internet, with millions of new sites being launched each year. How many packaging assignments were initiated last year? How many identity systems? How many posters? If I ask, "How many annual reports did your firm do last year?" my point should be clear enough.

121

I suspect that everyone who reads this has already arrived at this assessment of the current media situation and has either shifted focus to some degree or has concluded (along with my friend), "That's fine. There's enough design work to go around that we can let the Web firms do all the Web shit." That might be true. But here's my concern— and please keep in mind that I am a writer with an advertising background, not a designer.

I worry that in abdicating Web design to the specialists, a huge opportunity is being missed—maybe the biggest opportunity since magazines, books, album covers, and annual reports came along in the '60s, '70s, '80s, and '90s, respectively. The same homogeny of globalization that has affected advertising exists on the Web, and the only heroes I can see riding in to save the day are inspired graphic designers. Once the more sophisticated companies start figuring this out, Web site budgets should support just about any design firm's hourly rates. Mark Parker's recent announcement about shifting Nike's marketing dollars more toward the Web, then peeling away a significant portion of longtime partner Wieden+Kennedy's business to do just that, signals that the change is already happening.

Again, from my simplistic advertising copywriter perspective, it seems that the reasons some of my favorite designers have not fully committed to the Web include that:

They fundamentally don't want to.

They love things that they can touch, feel, and fondle.

They feel dictated to and limited by the technology.

But just as learning more about the printing process made better designers, it seems that learning more about what is and isn't possible in Web-land would also make better designers. Fortunately, the young bucks coming into your firms are Web-savvy. But I guess I still feel some reticence on the part of some of my favorite designers. Maybe I'm just bored with 99 percent of the Web sites I see, relative to some of the other work I see my favorite designers creating.

It also occurs to me that modernism was all about coming to terms with the realities of the existing modern world and wrangling all of the available disciplines to the core principles of logical, beautiful design.

Someone reminded me recently that we are now in the midst of a postmodern movement, which, to me, seems like nothing more than cynicism and ennui in the wake of the last major important movement. It strikes me that it might be time for a whole new movement: maybe it should be called neo-modernism. And maybe neo-modernism embraces the new machines.

Maybe you should be one of the fathers or mothers of this movement.

A NEW SECRET WEAPON FOR PRODUCING GREAT WORK: RESPECT

124

3.0 MIN.

I just read about an experiment conducted by a group of medical researchers who recorded hundreds of conversations between physicians and their patients. Half the doctors had been sued for malpractice, and half hadn't. The panel members found that they could identify which ones had been sued just on the basis of those conversations. There were some telltale signs: the doctors who had been sued spent an average of three minutes less with their patients than the doctors who had never been sued. The sued doctors were less likely to make orienting statements like, "First, I'm going to do this, and then, we're going to do that." The sued doctors were also less likely to engage in active listening with their patients. And they were less humorous. There was absolutely no difference in the amount or quality of information they gave their patients, just a difference in attitude and bedside manner. The researchers decided to take the experiment a step further by cutting the interviews down to twenty seconds and obscuring the audio so that the panel couldn't even hear what the doctors were saying but could only observe their manner, body language, expressions, and so on. They were still able to identify the doctors who had been sued with almost 100 percent accuracy based on those doctors' tendency not to listen to or show respect for their patients. (My wife works at Oregon Health Sciences University, and she confirms this: "It's not the crappy doctors who get sued, it's the good doctors with the crappy attitudes.")

The implication for creative people: it's not just about how talented we are or how great our work is; our long-term success depends on having repeated "at bats," and having repeated at bats depends on having satisfied clients, and having satisfied clients depends not just on producing great work but also on our attitude and bedside manner.

125

I have been fortunate to have enjoyed some exceptionally long-term client relationships. I had one client follow me through four different agency changes over a ten-year period. But I have also been guilty of prejudging clients and expecting the worst, especially when I see behavior that reminds me of another bad client experience. I'm not naïve enough to think that all clients are fundamentally good or smart or talented, but I also know that clients are necessary, unless I want to just focus on fine art, so I have to go in with respect and a willingness to really listen to them and their concerns.

I never make New Year's resolutions, but it happens that I'm pondering this during the first week of a new year. So, I'm pressing the reset button. I'm still interested in finding clients who are courageous and smart, and I'll still be cautious and turn away work if I don't think I can add value. But I'm making a choice to return to the wonder and exuberance of someone who gets paid by clients to do what he loves. And he happens to love producing great work.

HOW THE SAARINEN FAMILY ~~SAVED ME FROM BECOMING~~ ~~THE SAUSAGE KING~~

3.0 MIN.

It almost seemed like Manifest Destiny: I was born for meat-related greatness. My grandfather, my father and his three brothers, their wives, my cousin, my nephew, and my two half-brothers have all worked for the family business, Economy Sausage—at one time, quite the going concern in Canada. My father, Alfred Howe, was the one who wrote the amazing tagline that graced all manner of trucks, playing cards, ashtrays, and pencils: *The sausage that made little piggies famous.* Yup. That's the kind of genius DNA that I inherited. And I would have inherited a whole lot more if I had decided to go into pork products instead of advertising and design. (My only sibling also managed to escape by becoming a corporate attorney.)

There it was: the whole sausage world open before me, and yet my only fascinations at age seven and eight—much to my father's consternation and concern—were Moshe Safdie's Habitat 67 on the Marc-Drouin Quay in Montreal, the Monsanto House of the Future at Disneyland (which I was constantly drawing), Redline Hot Wheels (the purple Silhouette, in particular), certain advertisements (which I would clip out and file or hang on my bedroom wall), and, for some odd reason, Eero Saarinen's tulip table and chairs. There was also some weird obsession with royal blue carpeting (which I finally convinced my parents to let me have in my room), but I'll leave that to a professional psychotherapist to figure out.

These things—particularly Habitat, the House of the Future, and the tulip table and chairs—completely captured my imagination. I didn't think of them as being products of "modernism," because I wouldn't even process that term for several years. There was just something about those fluid, playful-yet-functional forms that rocked my world and haunted a small piece of real estate somewhere in my psyche right up until this moment.

129

But it was a happy haunting, because somehow, Eero Saarinen's voice spoke through his design directly to me, saying, in effect, "There is this beautiful, perfect vision out there that will bubble right up out of your personality, and it will have a lasting impact."

You know the Saarinens' story, I'm sure. A Finnish family that emigrated to the United States in the 1920s; architect dad Eliel taught at Cranbrook, where Eero studied sculpture and furniture design alongside Charles and Ray Eames, and where he befriended Florence Knoll. Eero went on to study architecture at Yale and eventually opened his own practice. In addition to projects like the Gateway Arch in St. Louis and the TWA Flight Center at JFK, he collaborated with Knoll on a number of furniture projects—including the tulip table and chairs in the late '50s. The iconic table and chairs are still in production, and, in my humble opinion, are still as "fluid and playful-yet-functional" today as they were when they were first introduced and when they first showed up on my radar. (Check them out at Design Within Reach [*www.DWR.com*].)

The point (in case you were worried that I didn't have one) is that your work—maybe not all of it, but the best of it—*speaks*. And it can speak over decades. It can speak to an eight-year-old boy and capture his imagination in such a way that it literally changes the course of his life. It can make him turn his back on "the sausage that made little piggies famous" and pursue a beautiful, perfect vision that bubbles right up out of his personality and (hopefully) has a lasting impact.

131

A WRITER'S VIEW OF SEMIOTICS AND WHY YOU MIGHT CARE

3.0 MIN.

One of my very favorite designers wrote, "Graphic design which fulfills aesthetic needs, complies with the laws of form and the exigencies of two-dimensional space; which speaks in semiotics, sans-serifs, and geometries; which abstracts, transforms, translates, rotates, dilates, repeats, mirrors, groups, and regroups, is not good design if it is irrelevant."

I have argued for more of you and less of your client, but this quote from Paul Rand's *Thoughts on Design* provides us with a sensible caveat. However, relevance can be skinned a couple of different ways.

There is intellectual relevance: "This idea makes sense to me and I agree or disagree with it."

And there is emotional relevance, which doesn't necessarily have a logical, intellectual framework at all, but communicates on a more visceral (and, I would argue, potentially more powerful) level.

But communicating with emotional relevance takes competency and skill—things Rand had. A designer operating at this level can preface an idea with all the analytic, bulletproof logic of a tax attorney, and then unveil the most abstract, counterintuitive idea that stuns us with its simplicity, beauty, and inevitability. Michael Bierut's redesign of Massimo Vignelli's identity for Saks is the most powerful example of this in recent memory. It communicates primarily at an emotional level. I was stopped dead in my tracks when I first discovered parts of it while walking past a Saks window display in Portland. Recently, I was on my way to a meeting with one of my favorite designers. We were both arrested by the exact same image simultaneously: a small section of

133

a black and white shopping bag sticking out of a bundle of curbside recycling. Without missing a beat, we looked at each other and said, "Michael Bierut."

Within the context of rampant media oversaturation, it strikes me that this kind of emotionally resonant communication has the greatest potential to stand out and connect with its intended audience, and to possibly even justify its own existence from a humane, aesthetic standpoint.

This point was further driven home to me early this morning while I was walking my dog in the park near our house. I was just waking up. The Stumptown hadn't quite kicked in yet, and my general morning fog allowed me to only process the bare minimum of signs, data, and input presented to me in those moments. Visually, I registered "green" (the grass was a brilliant green), "grass," "black" (Katie's shiny black coat), "dog," "brown" (the tree she was headed for was a majestic old growth fir), and "tree."

And that was it. *Green, grass, black, dog, brown,* and *tree.* Six bytes of information out of the potential millions (some physicists and biologists might put that number in the billions) of data points or atomic substructures visible or invisible to my human eye. I'm sure my senses would have discerned other data under normal circumstances. But these weren't particularly normal circumstances; I was tired. And that, I submit, is precisely the state of our audience today: Tired. Weary. Over-targeted. Under-respected.

Given this, we have to help our clients prioritize and empathize. What is the key bit of communication here that may actually help or inform our audience in some way? What is its "green?" What is its "grass?"

Its "black?" All the other details will fall away, anyway, so we might as well serve up the key information with emotional relevance.

I was reading Marinetti's *Futurist Manifesto* this week, and it struck me how this document was as poetic and abstract as it was incendiary and revolutionary. It provoked. It challenged. It was intended to shake up the tired, bourgeois art of its time.

I am becoming more and more convinced that nothing is as powerful as relevant abstraction. It's what we all strive for and rarely achieve: a kind of poetry to our work, but poetry that incites, stirs, and even shocks.

MY LUNCH WITH MICHELLE PFEIFFER AND WHATSHISNAME

4.0 MIN.

On my Web site, I list some of my heroes and influences. If forced to edit that list down to three or four "super" heroes, Jay Chiat would have to be on the shorter list.

Chiat is the founder of the agency that eventually became TBWA \ Chiat \ Day, and in the 1980s and early '90s, there was no hotter agency on the planet. This heat emanated from what was then the most unlikely locale, geographically speaking: Los Angeles. Madison Avenue was, well, the Madison Avenue of advertising, with Chicago and possibly London following in tow. Chiat, a New Yorker by birth, managed to buck this trend and do things on his own terms. He set up office on the second floor of the Biltmore Hotel in downtown L.A., and later moved the agency—along with the entire advertising and production communities (they usually follow the agencies)—to Venice Beach, in a groundbreaking workspace designed by his friend and fellow iconoclast, Frank Gehry. That space was the "Binocular Building."

Back to the '80s for a second. To the Biltmore. There, under one roof, were Jay, Lee Clow, Steve Hayden, Rick Boyko, Bill Hamilton, Tom Cordner, Jeff Gorman, Gary Johns, and Wieden+Kennedy's future CEO Dave Luhr: a veritable Who's Who of advertising. Oh, and then there was the client roster: Nike (who decided to stray from Wieden for its television ads and Olympics effort), Apple (you might remember a certain TV ad introducing the Macintosh), Porsche, Pioneer, Pizza Hut, Yamaha, California Cooler—and they dominated every awards competition.

In the mid-'90s, after winning global chores for Nissan, Chiat began looking for an international network to service the massive account. Some believed that he was simply looking for a way to cash out.

However, Chiat \ Day remained strong (creatively) under Clow's passionate, watchful eye, even as the agency attempted an ill-fated merger with Australia-based Mojo. By the time TBWA came calling, Jay was withdrawing from the day-to-day business of his firm, occupying himself with his growing art collection, and consulting with some Internet start-ups. That's when I called him. Or, to be more precise, that's when I asked my account guy, Michael Niles (who had worked at Chiat \ Day during its glory days), to call him. Having sold my agency, I was now exploring the possibilities that existed within the broader world of communications, which would ultimately lead me to the conclusion that design and advertising needed to fuse and that I needed to be part of that fusion. However, at this point, I merely sought an audience with someone whose vision and leadership and chutzpah had been a searchlight for me, and to my delight, he agreed to meet for lunch at the Ivy at the Shore in Santa Monica. I had met Jay a few years earlier in New York, but we didn't really have a chance to chat. Now, I was going to have his undivided attention.

I flew down for the day and decided that it would be appropriate (this being Jay Chiat and all) to upgrade my rental car to a fancy convertible (a Jaguar, as I recall). When I pulled up to the Ivy, Jay was pulling up, as well—in a decidedly un-fancy Toyota. We exchanged greetings and sat down. After ordering iced teas and making some small talk about what was going on at the agency bearing his name, I decided to launch into some of the big, lofty, visionary questions I had been dying to ask him. That's when she walked in and sat directly across from me. I remembered someone telling me once that Michelle Pfeiffer was far more beautiful in person than she was on screen, but that is one of those incidental

138

bits of trivia you just tuck away. I wasn't even a big Michelle Pfeiffer fan. Until this moment. She was stunning, and she was sitting directly across from me.

For the next ninety minutes, my advertising guru waxed eloquent about the future of advertising and communications, and I am absolutely certain that he dropped some serious insight bombs that would have changed the course of my career—and probably the course of communications as we know them—forever, except that I wasn't paying attention to a single word Jay was saying. My range of focus was limited to: Michelle Pfeiffer. Beautiful. There.

I thanked Jay for his time, we shook hands and wished each other well, and I headed back to the airport. Now, you might be wondering what possible lesson there is to be gleaned from such an intensely personal anecdote. Just this: sometimes, beautiful design can actually be more compelling than pure content; in fact, sometimes, beautiful design can actually *become* content. Jay = content. Michelle = beautiful design. In this particular media environment (the Ivy), beautiful design trumped pure content. (The other lesson: always rent the subcompact.)

FOR EVERY CAVEMAN, THERE'S A TALKING GECKO

3.0 MIN.

Back in 1998, the Martin Agency presented a new advertising campaign to the Government Employees Insurance Company (GEICO), which was hoping to make a splash on national television. The campaign featured a reptilian mascot. More specifically, a gecko. (Get it? GEICO… GECKO?) Just what every advertiser dreams of: a memorable mnemonic in the tradition of the equally inspired Aflac (sounds-like-duck-quack). How much do I hate the GEICO gecko commercials? I will dive across the room to change the channel. I hope they end up in the same special corner of hell where Sleep Country U.S.A. and Shane Company commercials play on an endless loop. What makes the gecko ads so reprehensible is that they're not cheap to produce; they're created by the same animation house responsible for the *Harry Potter* movies. Worse still, this is the same client (roughly) responsible for approving the mildly entertaining celebrity-assisted testimonials currently airing. But here is the irony that could only exist in advertising: this same client (again, I'm not certain if it was the exact same client group within GEICO) was also responsible for what is, in my opinion, one of the high points of commercial television advertising—ever.

Sometime in 2005, the first of three new GEICO commercials aired—without our slimy green friend. An innocuous spokesperson in a suit and tie delivers a brief and simple pitch: handling your insurance online at Geico.com is so easy, even a caveman could do it. Cut to an upscale restaurant, where we now see the GEICO spokesperson apologizing… and you know the rest. I'm not sure that I've seen a better comedic performance in any commercial before or since.

There have been several hilarious caveman commercials since, including one with a psychotherapist played by two-time Oscar nominee Talia Shire

(*The Godfather, Rocky*), as well as an ill-fated attempt at spinning them off and making the premise into a series. The advertising gods did not smile on this endeavor. But they most certainly did smile on that first caveman commercial, which, to me, orbits in the same rarefied air as Apple's *1984*, Volkswagen's *Funeral*, Alka-Seltzer's *I Can't Believe I Ate the Whole Thing*, the California Fluid Milk Processors' *Aaron Burr—Got Milk?* and Honda's *Cog*. These are rare and magical moments (and certainly there are more to list) when advertising ceases to be advertising. When the strategy, the writing, the design, the casting, the direction, and the execution have all been boiled down to such beautiful simplicity that it elevates the piece to something more akin to an installation on film. Many of these commercials have been directed by accomplished feature film directors: for example, Ridley Scott for *1984*, Michael Bay for *Aaron Burr—Got Milk?*

Back to GEICO for a second. I will forgive the stupid gecko for one reason and one reason only: the company approved two pissed-off cavemen sitting in an upscale restaurant, giving a GEICO spokesperson some serious attitude. I am physically unable to watch the caveman commercial without laughing my ass off. I forgive them for their spotty judgment; however, if they were to do more commercials like the one I just cited, and do away altogether with the reptile, I would seriously consider calling them and switching insurance companies.

(Something tells me that my Farmers agent need not worry.)

EVEN WHEN WE'RE LYING WE'RE TELLING THE TRUTH

144

8.0 MIN.

I want to share a conceptual "trick" I've learned over these many years of attempting to turn data into a singular and (hopefully) inspired idea—one that I can ultimately hang a narrative on—in a relatively compressed amount of time (usually relative to the backbone of the project manager or account person on that particular job). The trick is actually a system that the world's best actors employ.

Constantin Stanislavski is arguably the most important figure in the history of acting-as-storytelling. He referred to his approach as "spiritual realism," but actors generally refer to his system simply as the Method or as Method acting. I like his own handle better because it gets at the core of powerful storytelling: *telling the truth and removing every obstacle to telling that truth*. Try this in your car, ideally when you're alone: Say out loud, "I don't want to see anyone until I'm clean." It's a line from *Things We Lost in the Fire*. In the film, Benicio Del Toro (who might be one of our generation's best Method actors) removes every obstacle to telling the truth about Jerry, a recovering heroin addict. My guess-slash-prediction is that you won't be very convincing when you say the line the first time. Or the second time. Or the third. You will hear yourself say the words, but you won't believe it. It won't sound "true," because it isn't. (Unless it is, in which case I would strongly urge you to pull over and seek help immediately.)

We just know when something feels true.

One of the amazing things about dreams is that our brain can call on all kinds of inputs, memories, people, places, and even multiple timelines and somehow synthesize them into a (temporarily) cohesive narrative. It somehow makes total and complete sense that we are back in high

145

school driving on a freeway in Canada and carrying on a perfectly normal conversation with Kate Moss and Pete Doherty, who are on a completely different freeway in England, about which hand lotion is best—especially when we wake up suddenly to find our dog, Katie, licking our hand, which is hanging off the side of the bed. Our brain is working hard to find a narrative from all the inputs, internal and external. It is trying to find the truth.

One of Stanislavski's tricks was to turn a mistake into an opportunity to build on a scripted narrative and create a deeper level of truth. For example, two actors are sitting at a table talking. One actor accidentally knocks a box of Kleenex onto the floor. A technical actor will either just ignore the Kleenex or pick it up and put it back on the table, self-consciously: we're suddenly taken completely (and hopefully temporarily) out of the moment. Another, deeper level of truth has come into play. A Method actor, on the other hand, lives for these moments. He might kick the box across the room if he is frustrated in the scene, or pick it up and blow his nose and maybe offer it to the other actor. Suddenly, that "mistake" has become an input that transports us into the reality of the scene. Just as our brain integrates the licking of our hand with a discussion about hand lotion in our dream, an unexpected accident can lead to a very interesting area at which we might not have arrived on our own.

When I am working on a project, I spend an inordinate amount of time reading and rereading the brief, going over the existing research, and looking at the client's Web site, past advertising—whatever I can get my hands on. That's tantamount to Method actors doing their homework about a character. Once I have a halfway decent sense of what the brief is and who the character (brand) is, I start writing statements and stories about the brand. This is just for me, not necessarily to be shared with anyone except my design partners. But I won't even share it with them until I have arrived at a few statements or stories that feel true about the brand, about the category, or even about the consumer.

At this stage, it is never about whether the client will buy or agree with what I've written. It is only about what seems true to me. This is where I think a lot of creative people get off track: they start worrying about what will or won't fly with their clients or their internal teams way too early in the process, and they start building on that shaky, often illogical, and fundamentally untrue foundation. There will be plenty of time to deal with client biases, politics, mandatories, and obstacles later. For now, we should only be concerned with what's true. Once we've arrived at what the core truth or truths are, we are free to work from a place of reality. Count on it: the Kleenex box will fall off the table at some point. But instead of being freaked out by client interference or middle management fears or budget issues or the sudden revelation that we are required to use existing photography, we must integrate it into the truth of the situation. We might decide to kick the existing photography across the room in frustration or use it to blow our nose, but at least we're doing it out of a basis of truth about the client and about the communication.

When I have failed on a project, it has usually been as a result of not establishing the truth up front. An actor's raw talent can only carry him so far. If he doesn't have a baseline of truth about his character, he's at the mercy of the director, the producer, the studio executives, and—apparently—Lily Tomlin. The same holds true for a director, perhaps more so—since a director has to track the truth and character arcs of the entire ensemble.

147

One final thought about the truth: even when we lie, we are trying to tell the truth. We're trying to convince others—and more often ourselves— of a different narrative than that which seems obvious in a given situation. That's why bald-faced lies sometimes seem more believable than half-truths. My favorite *SNL* character of recent years is Kristen Wiig's Penelope, who shows up at various functions twirling her hair and one-upping everyone who speaks with her ridiculous claims. A lady's cat has just died, and guest host Molly Shannon comments that the cat was just like a child to her. Penelope says, "My cat was my child, I was pregnant with my cat, I gave birth to it, so ... I had my cat baby in the hospital and had a cat baby shower, so ... " In some of the sketches, her claims seem so bizarre ("I can make myself invisible, so ...), but as everyone leaves in disgust, she actually becomes invisible.

So, I guess what I'm trying to say is, get to the truth first. And then: lie your ass off.

WHAT IS MODERN?

7.0 MIN.

I recently posed the question to a handful of my favorite designers:
"What is 'modern' today?"

I am cautious about drifting too deeply into the dark waters of design
theory or criticism—especially given that I am not a practicing graphic
designer (creative director, writer, advocate, and cheerleader—but *not*
designer). So, the only authority I can claim on the subject is my passion
for it, some experience working alongside a few of the top designers in
the country, and my primary interest in *ideas*. The beauty—or perhaps
the folly—of my particular point of view is that it is (almost) totally naive.
That is to say, I am aware that there are scholars at places like Cranbrook,
CalArts, and Art Center who have forgotten more than I will ever know
about graphic design, modernism, or any other "ism" associated with
our profession. This is a discussion in which I can claim (or disclaim)
with 100 percent confidence: I am a copywriter and a Canadian, and
I might be wrong.

This particular idea of what constitutes "modern" interests me on
a number of levels. First, that there is even a relevant discussion to be
had at all, after nearly eight decades, especially given the nature of
some of the people discussing it. "To an artist," someone pointed out,
"Modernism is about rebellion." But a rebel generally rejects any kind
of "ism" or man-made code as arbitrary and doctrinaire. Artists generally
view rules as things to be broken, and yet your own responses and the
writings and lectures of respected designers and architects still betray
a respect—almost a reverence—for the teachings and the motivations of
the Bauhaus and its graphic heir, European modernism.

151

One of my favorite designers referenced Charles Eames' perspective that modernism is about being true to your times, that it involves using the tools and methods at the forefront of your generation to create things that are a genuine reflection of that particular point in time. I agree that this was a major tenet of the movement, but I don't see that as the prevailing principle of design *today*. Some of our most talented designers are still loath to embrace the design opportunities presented by the Web, which—along with portable media players and Internet-enabled cellular phone technology—would have to constitute "the tools and methods at the forefront" of our generation.

From my "fly on the wall" perspective from working with design firms in different parts of the country, I see a kind of pluralism: a search for new forms here, a return to old forms there. At some level, possibly even a subconscious one, I think many designers are struggling to determine whether the principles of modernism still apply. The one area where this confusion has been most prevalent is in typography.

Obviously, every person engaged in the applied arts has a right and a responsibility to explore new approaches, new forms, even new combinations of old forms. On the surface, it seems like the design community should always be asking the question, "What's next?" But I would submit that a more meaningful and useful question to ask is, "What's true?" Asking, "What's next?" leads to trendy (as in temporary or dated—not as in relevant or culturally aware), to superficial style-over-substance, to sameness, even to blatant copying. I think asking, "What's true?" leads to smart, fresh, powerful, and classic. The kind of classic that makes nearly all of Josef Müller-Brockmann's posters, and pretty much everything Paul Rand did, look like it could have been done today (assuming there was someone capable of doing work like that today). Another one of my favorite designers recently showed me a gem he found at Powell's: a fifty-five-year-old book called *The Candidate*, about Jimmy Durante's tongue-in-cheek bid for the presidency in 1952. I have no idea who designed this wonderful little artifact, but it's as fresh and beautiful and elegant as anything you'll see in this year's CA Design Annual. Or next year's.

When I ask, "What's true?" I conclude that many of the enduring principles of modernism (and the new typography) are still relevant today because they were (and are) fundamentally true. (True as in "laws"—such as gravitation or thermodynamics—not as in "rules.") If you are constantly questioning and trying to break rules, you are probably an artist. If you are constantly questioning and trying to break laws, you are probably an idiot.

Which brings me to postmodernism and its bastard child, deconstructionism, the so-called New Wave, *Émigré*, *Beach Culture*, *Ray Gun*, and all the other "movements" that were supposed to signal the end of modernism as we know it. I subscribed to *Émigré*, even bought a bunch of the fonts (which, even at the time, I thought of as "novelty fonts" like Hobo and Dom Casual), but the interesting thing is that I don't see any of those fonts that were going to change our idea of legibility being used by any of my favorite designers today. And I think my last issue of *Émigré* showed up sometime around 2001. Gone. Randy VanderLans, Zuzana Licko, April Greiman, and David Carson are all still relatively young, and yet (ostensibly) gone. I'm not hating here, I'm simply pointing out what seems obvious to a Canadian copywriter who didn't go to art school: that the reports of the death of modernism are greatly exaggerated.

153

Classic, legible typography is alive and well, and perhaps enjoying even greater usage today, given the breakneck pace of our digitized culture and the predominance of e-mails and text messaging.

The bottom line is that times change, culture changes, and tastes change, but great ideas will always be great ideas. They will stand the test of time. And insofar as graphic design is about ideas first and foremost, and as long as the execution serves the idea, it really doesn't matter what we call it or how academia tries to reverse engineer it. A great idea that Massimo Vignelli created for a department store logo in 1973 is still a great idea today. And a great idea that Michael Bierut creates for that same department store in 2007 will be a great idea in 2041.

Another one of my very favorite designers whose work you would definitely recognize (but not from annuals, because he refuses to enter award shows) has only a handful of fonts that he goes to. Far from being rigid or stylistically redundant, he is one of the most flexible and open-minded problem-solvers I have ever worked with. And his work is always highly conceptual, fresh, and, well, *modern.*

Some of the principles of modernism that I would submit have survived the test of time are the importance of design itself to society, the importance of an interdisciplinary approach to design, the importance of logic, the importance of legibility in typography, the importance of respecting the "end user" (not exactly a 1930s term, but probably a more updated way of thinking about functionalism), the importance of simple and elegant beauty without unnecessary adornment (see

154

respect for end user and functionalism), the importance of materials and utilizing the latest tools and technologies available, and—probably most importantly—the importance of ideas.

WHAT MAKING RADIO COMMERCIALS TAUGHT ME ABOUT DESIGN

5.0 MIN.

I was one of those weird advertising copywriters who actually liked writing and producing radio commercials. While my creative cohorts jostled over TV briefs, I would take the lowly radio brief, hole myself up in my office, and try to make something special out of it. Occasionally, I did. Seeing a huge need-slash-opportunity to reinvent a tired and underutilized category, I launched *Radioland* in 1996. We had offices in Portland and Los Angeles, and I eventually opened a recording studio called The Big What If in Hollywood. For the next several years, with the exception of the occasional design writing assignment, I focused exclusively on radio advertising. I got to work with all of my favorite agencies (Wieden, Crispin, Chiat, Deutsch, and an endless blur of other, lesser-known agencies), helping them creative direct, write, cast, direct, and produce their radio campaigns. Most of my friends just wanted to know why. Why would I ostensibly abandon the traditional advertising agency world to go make … *radio commercials*? The answer was almost disappointingly simple: The audio medium is all about the story. In the absence of visuals, the writing and sound design of the commercial have to somehow evoke the visual experience for the listener. That's why I liked storyboarding radio ads. It helped me guide listeners through the narrative, visually. They're going to see *something*, I reasoned. Might as well try to manage that a bit. (Once the visual story line is managed, you can really start messing with the listener.)

There was something about telling stories using only sound that felt remarkably similar to the design process. To start with, there was the importance of the idea itself. So many writers fool themselves into thinking they have an idea just because they have a script. That's why I always require writers or creative teams to bring their raw ideas

157

first—before they present scripts. If they can't get me (or themselves) excited about the kernel of an idea, then the script won't save it. When I consult agencies or do workshops, I encourage creative people not to ask themselves what they want a particular piece of communication to *say*, but what they want it to *do*. I think the same applies to any great piece of design.

The other bit of wisdom I gained from doing a few hundred radio ads is the importance of having one singular message. Managing a client's expectations up front is the key here. I do an exercise with new clients who want to venture out onto the airwaves: I ask them what commercials they can remember hearing during the past week. Usually, they can't remember a single one, or if they do, it's one that was particularly grating. On the rare occasion that someone does remember a good ad, I ask them what they remember about that ad. They can usually only remember one or maybe two things, if that. Then, I remind them that advertisers are still spending hundreds of millions of dollars each year on radio advertising, and all they (marketing types, usually more attuned to advertising) can remember is one or two things from one or two ads. That typically serves as a bit of a sobering wake-up call. How do they expect their ads to fare any better? How many of those six vital copy points do they think people will remember in a week's time? Maybe there are some corollaries to posters or printed pieces in this.

There was one other real-world lesson that radio taught me about graphic design. In some ways, actors are like typography, music is like color, concept is like photography or illustration, and writing is akin to layout. At times, the concept was dictated by the agency or client to some degree. Other times, the writing was already approved when

158

it arrived on my desk. I could choose to turn down the job (which I did probably more times than I should have), or take the job and try to improve upon it as much as humanly possible (which I did probably more times than I should have). I suspect that you have done both, as well. In the absence of an amazing, singular idea, going in with less-than-inspired writing, I would attempt to make those thirty to sixty seconds as much a gift to the listener as I could. I spent countless hours agonizing over casting (typography), I begged favors and wore myself out trying to find up-and-coming musicians to create original music or reinvent an existing piece of stock music (color), and I protected and nurtured and terrorized and surprised the actors to elicit the best, most interesting performances from them. The whole process required all of my diplomatic skills (which are severely limited), plus my ability to coerce, convince, argue, beg, plead, and pout—just to get something good produced. Again, I suspect that you've been *there*, as well.

"Consolation for humanity through art." That was Vincent Van Gogh's stated mission, and that was the approach I took to radio. That was also the approach I took to print and television and outdoor: doing everything with the end goal of providing gifts to the intended receiver. A few years ago, I decided that there was more consolation for humanity in great design than there was in advertising (the exception being design firms doing great advertising), so I only do the odd radio commercial now (the odder the better). I served as the CLIOSs radio jury chairman a couple of years ago and judged the One Show's radio entries in 2008. But my primary focus now is singular: helping my favorite graphic designers tell stories. And that has provided consolation for at least *one* human.

159

THE IMPORTANCE OF PRESENTATION SKILLS

7.0 MIN.

On a scale of one to ten, one being worst and ten being ace, how good of a presenter do you think you are? Up until about a year ago, I would have rated myself an eight or a nine. I prided myself on this particular skill set and felt I had accumulated enough positive feedback over the years to substantiate this high a rating. I remember George Lois saying that "two-thirds of being a creative person is selling and protecting your ideas" (this from a man who once threatened to jump out of his clients' window if they didn't approve his poster design). Well, times have changed since then, and the mass exodus of marginal creative talent to the relative security of in-house creative positions has made "collaboration" and "creative problem solving" the norm for design firms and for advertising agencies. This has necessitated a whole new set of presentation skills— a far more democratic approach. But human nature hasn't changed since Lois perched himself on that window ledge. Great ideas still do not entirely sell themselves, because people will always naturally gravitate to the known, the tried, the tested.

I remember distinctly the first time I realized that I was a halfway decent presenter. I was working on a campaign that had to be presented to a client in New Jersey, but for some reason, we weren't able to go there to present in person, so we videotaped the presentation instead of just sending them the boards. After I made the presentation, I watched the video to see if I had covered all the crucial points. In real time, while I was presenting, I remember feeling nervous, a little self-conscious, and unsure of whether or not I was doing the work justice. My mouth was a little dry, my knees were a tad weak—the usual. But when I watched it, none of that came through. I remember thinking, "Geez, that's pretty good, Austin. *I'd* buy what you're selling." (As it turned out, the client

161

felt the same way.) That's why I always urge creative people to watch videotapes of their presentations. More often than not, it encourages them rather than exposing massive flaws in their presentation style. Sure, there are distracting little tics and idiosyncrasies that come up, but they can be corrected with practice. Unless they're completely out of touch, people generally do a better job of presenting than they think they're doing at the time. If you'd score yourself a five or less, and you've never watched yourself present, I encourage you to have someone film you presenting some time and then watch it. You might be surprised.

I mentioned that I have revised my assessment of my presenting skills over the past year. As I turned my attention to this apparent shift, two things became clear: one, the world of advertising and design has changed dramatically over the past decade, to a much more democratic, collaborative model. Gone are the days of the lone ranger (i.e., Lois) going off to work in isolation, coming back to present his "big idea," and then defending it to the death. Concepting has become much more of a group effort. I'm not entirely sure it's better, but it's reality. Secondly, I realized that my emphasis on broadcast (primarily radio) over the past ten years has made me an expert at presenting radio campaigns. I had enough practice that I became extremely good at it. But then, it was relatively easy to master: you do five to ten minutes (at the most) of setup, and then you present a script (a script that—in most cases—you yourself have written and labored over and rehearsed in your head countless times). That and a little bit of acting skill generally resulted in applause, laughter, and client approval. More importantly, I did this enough times (I tried to count—maybe a thousand different presentations) that I learned how to shut up after presenting and let the game come to me. In other words, there is only a certain number of client reactions possible, and I became adept at fielding almost every concern. As a result, I was able to get some pretty challenging ideas through some otherwise tough clients. Sometimes, the challenge became getting—or sometimes keeping—a controversial spot on the air.

Fast forward to 2008. I'm presenting a pretty thorough and impassioned proposal to a design firm on how it can take things to the next level— basically, a rebranding effort. One of the partners informs me that he has a client emergency that he needs to attend to and we may have to keep things short. In retrospect, I should have rescheduled or suggested that we wait until we could go off-site for a half day to cover all the material I had to present. Instead, I jumped in at a breakneck pace and tried to cover everything in about an hour. I was excited about the content (ideas), but I'm pretty sure I just overwhelmed my listeners with the volume of information. They seemed impressed with the presentation, but I left that meeting feeling like crap because I wasn't letting the game come to me. And then I thought of several other presentations over the past year in which I was pretty sure I'd overwhelmed my audience with exuberance and information. Rather than sit and lick my self-inflicted wounds, I decided to step back and assess my approach. I asked a few close friends and colleagues for honest feedback on my presenting and decided to employ the services of a presentation skills coach. The upshot of the feedback I received may or may not be helpful to you, but it definitely gave me some things to work on.

My first epiphany was the radio thing: that I had come close to mastering a certain *kind* of presentation, and that it was time for a new learning curve. Because now, I found myself not just presenting a relatively small

163

slice of an overall program, but often being tasked with presenting the entire program. This gave me a new appreciation for the awesome account planners and account executives that I had worked with (and leaned heavily upon) over the years.

The next revelation was the idea of *transference*, courtesy of one of my favorite designers. Since we had made several presentations in tandem (including a speech to a group of advertising and design students), he had seen me in action on a number of occasions. His feedback was that my passion for ideas is great but relentless— that maybe I should present the ideas with my usual passion and then sit back and let the clients get excited about them. In other words, let the work … *work*. Or, trust the work a bit more. (I have tried that on a few occasions since with remarkable results.)

Another useful bit of feedback had to do with preparation. Not the *amount* of preparation, necessarily, but the *nature* of that preparation. In other words, I need to envision the presentation in more realistic terms, taking into account potential client feedback and interaction. This necessitates editing the content down to its core essence, and again, trusting the material that I'm presenting. Because that is the art of what I do—the ideas. Not the presentation itself.

George Lois' economics of what it means to be a creative person (one-third ideas, two-thirds selling and protecting those ideas) may not hold up in today's market. To the extent that they do, I think this implies a smarter, more strategic approach to presentation—an approach that involves the kind of confidence that I felt presenting radio ideas.

164

That I can let the game come to me and I'll be able to deal with client pushback when it happens. And, as always, the realization that I might, in the final analysis, be wrong.

CONCEPT DEVELOPMENT: SOME DIFFERENT APPROACHES THAT WORK

9.5 MIN.

It suddenly occurred to me while I was writing this that some people might be uncomfortable with me pulling back the curtain a little bit, taking away some of the mystery (read: profitability) of their Super-Proprietary® approach. "Our ideation process is so much more sophisticated (and Proprietary® and profitable) than that." So, to put these folks at ease, I will state right up front that I am talking about my own personal process more than I am the creative processes or inner workings of the design or advertising firms that I work with. That said, I have had the unique opportunity to work with more than fifty different firms as a freelancer, and I can tell you that processes do not vary widely from one place to the next. There are slight differences from person to person in terms of individual creative processes, but that seems to me to be inevitable— even if two different designers took the exact same classes from the exact same professors and used the exact same black sketchbooks.

Things get a little more interesting (and, occasionally, awkward, at first) when two creative people with very different approaches come together to attack the same problem. It becomes a bit of a dance, except that unlike many dances that could be considered universal (the waltz is generally understood across many languages and cultures), we find ourselves changing our steps, alternating who is leading, and creating whole new expressions. Of course, sometimes it just doesn't work and toes get bruised, but that usually has more to do with attitude than approach. My favorite way to approach a creative problem is as follows, and I stress that this is my own preferred approach, and the ideal situation. Rarely do the stars align quite like this.

For starters, I don't like nice clients. Wait, let me rephrase that: I don't *trust* nice clients. I prefer tough ones who aren't there necessarily to be my buddy, but to collaborate and do something truly great. I don't like sugarcoating, and if a client uses the term "brilliant" or "genius," I know we're probably headed for trouble. That said, a respect for the creative process is a bonus—I just don't want to be patronized and pimped. If you love the work, then don't go on and on about it with us; go fall on your sword for it in front of your superiors. Sell it through. That's the loudest and most meaningful praise that any client can ever offer. So, let's say that we now have a tough (but fair) client who takes this whole thing seriously. I want to know everything about the company and about the products it provides. I want to know how it started and why. I want to know the strengths and maybe even the weaknesses of the founding partners and of the key stakeholders. I want to know why the company builds its products the way it does and how it's different from the way competitors do it. I want to spend a day at the facility, getting a sense of the vibe there and talking to "the guys in the white coats" (the makers). I want to look at every piece of communication the company has ever generated—as many as can be found. Eventually, I'll want to see what their competitors have done, but for now, I'd like to see how this brand has been talking to the world. I'll print out its entire Web site and tape every page to my walls (which gets interesting when I'm working on several projects at once). While this sounds like the regimen for working with a start-up, it's actually more meaningful to take this thorough approach with established brands—we take so much for granted, and by treating this little soft drink brand like it's just starting out, we can arrive at a much fresher and more meaningful take on a brand like Coca-Cola, for instance. There will be plenty of time for us to get inundated with all the rules and globally systematized standards that come with a brand that is a household name. But for now, and for the sake of creativity, this is almost a pro bono job.

Now is a good time to sit down with a designer. review the brief, and ask each other questions about what this whole thing is really all about. That begins as a friendly debate or tandem exploration. Discussions at this stage are generally aimed at getting our heads around precisely what the brief is all about, and what the company is all about. We talk about our interactions with this brand or others like it. We sit and think, sometimes for long periods. Questions are asked. Notes are jotted down. Semi-relevant doodles are drawn. We may be hungry at this point and decide to take the discussion to a restaurant, so the problem at hand moves to the back burner and we chat about other projects we're working on or about things we're reading. At some point in the meal, the conversation returns to the brief. "Is it *this*…?" one of us might ask. "Hmm," the other may respond, their mouth full of Reuben. More notes. More doodles. We head back to the studio. Now, thoughts are flowing a little more freely, and we start to challenge the brief in its various components. In most cases, unless we are working with a particularly inspired strategist, we begin to deconstruct the brief, question it, and recraft it. This can take a day or more. We finish off the workday by visiting the strategist or account person responsible for the brief and raising some of the issues that came up while we were picking the brief apart. They clarify and confirm, and we head home convinced that our basic assumptions are probably correct. The next day, we reconvene, both with completely different notions of what the assignment is and what the brand is all about. Debate ensues—healthy debate. Then, shards of ideas start to break through, and we write them down furiously. We start batting ideas back and forth like some kind of cerebral tennis match. In our heightened state, we misunderstand some of what the other is saying, and our rejoinders are actually a lot more interesting than if we had understood each other in the first place. Taglines or headlines or visuals start filling our books. For me, it's usually posters or wild postings. I always like to think in terms of visually taking over a city. Or, if it's a packaging assignment, I'll go stand in a retail store for a while and just study the best and worst packaging—whatever stands out. Then, I typically like to defer to whatever my designer's process is at this stage. Basically, it's time for them to go off and play, and it's probably time for me to work on some sort of treatise or manifesto for the brand, to see if I can sidle up to it and find its voice.

Some of the designers I work with require (or prefer) less involvement from me at this point; others use me as a sounding board all the way through. Because we both wrestle with the core attributes and essence of the brand, there is a kind of recognition when we hit on something that really reflects it. Together, we both just seem to know. Occasionally, I have a question or suggestion that might nudge them further down one path or another, but once there is a direction (or two or three) that we're feeling good about, I will set about writing a rationale or setup for each direction and help my designer partner craft the presentation itself so that it's basically bulletproof. Lately, some of my designer partners have been feeling their oats in terms of developing the manifesto. It used to be that just providing one for them was a revelation; now they're a lot more engaged in the writing process, for two reasons: one, this will be the brand map we follow, and it is sure to inform the design direction; and two, there is more ownership—both ways—over every piece of the process. I might be as vocal about a font as my partner is about a verb, but that's only because I'm a design geek. Nonetheless, I think it's really healthy—to a point. I am, after all, not Massimo Vignelli. Full stop.

In many cases, I find that taking the client through the brand manifesto first is a great way to get its head nodding in the right direction. It also helps do away with any "us versus them" barriers. After the manifesto, it's all "us." Then, the designer(s) will share the directions, with me chiming in as a "neutral third party." "I love this one because … "seems to have more weight because I'm not the one who designed it, and also because I have just finished waxing eloquent about their brand in a way that they probably couldn't.

I love being involved in identity systems, because I believe the best identity systems are always the most logical and strategic ones. And it seems to me that teaming a writer up with a designer on an identity project makes as much or more sense than teaming them up on an ad or poster or Web site.

Some designers have their own processes, which have worked for them, and they're loath to change or alter them in any significant way. That's fine with me. As I have said before, I find most designers to be pretty good writers in terms of editing text down to only the most necessary words and sentiments. But when there is collaboration and both of us are struggling to discover the truth and the inspiration within a brief, there are few experiences more satisfying than arriving at that "Aha!" moment

171

together. (Maybe actually *selling through* that "Aha!" moment to a tough but fair client.) There is more mischief with two. There's no such thing as a one-man conspiracy.

I don't look at awards annuals or other trade pubs when I'm concepting. But I will flip through magazines or photographers' books. I'm occasionally inspired by some of the work in *New American Paintings*. I do have a stupid little exercise that I do on almost every job, especially broadcast jobs: I call it the pun test. Once we've got a handle on an inspired strategy, I make a list of every pun or play on words or cliché around that basic idea, just to see if those thoughts spark any other thoughts. For instance, if the strategy is, say, "For men who love shoes a little too much," I would make a list of related thoughts, like:

> You can do anything, but stay off of my blue suede shoes.
>
> You can never have too many shoes.
>
> Imelda Marcos > Imelda's husband.
>
> Men who love too much.
>
> How do I love thee? Let me count the ways.
>
> Walk a mile in my shoes > (Don't even think about walking) a mile in my shoes.
>
> There was an old woman who lived in a shoe > There was an old *man* who lived in a shoe.

And so on. Inter-relationships and connections can lead to unexpected, slightly more abstract ideas. Visual ideas. Like this last line from the old nursery rhyme. You can start to visualize what the shoe might look like as a bachelor pad, what kind of shoe it would be, how clean and tastefully appointed it would be, and suddenly, we have a conflict because the story goes on to tell of the old woman having so many children that she didn't know what to do. A guy who loves shoes a little too much would know exactly what to do: jettison the kids and add mid-century furniture, tasty flower arrangements, groovy Verner Panton "tongue," and a white shag instep.

Of course, sometimes even the most creative individuals occasionally need an edge, and that's when mind-expanding drugs may be necessary. (Like Stumptown. Or, only in the gravest cases, Mountain Dew.)

SEVEN DESIGNER SHADES OF GRAY

7.0 MIN.———————

~~WHICH DRUGS WORK BEST FOR DIFFERENT KINDS OF PROJECTS?~~

6.0 MIN.

Clearly, there are times when even our best efforts fall short of brilliance. At these crucial points, it's important to at least be aware of our options. Since this is not a topic generally covered in most design school curricula, I'll approach it from a slightly more academic angle. But hopefully, you'll leave this essay with a better handle on the tools available to you as a designer—particularly in those moments when inspiration just can't be found.

Let's start with the design equivalent of "writer's block." You're stuck. The heavens are brass. Nothing is coming and you're tempted to just procrastinate on this one assignment, unconsciously electing to leverage the inevitable adrenalin rush that comes from a looming deadline to tackle it. It's certainly a tried-and-true method—I have used it myself, many times. But there are at least two downsides to this last-minute adrenalin rush approach: one, you may get another assignment in the interim—also with a tight deadline—that will minimize the amount of time you'll be able to spend on the problem assignment. Two, you may find yourself just as stuck as before, but now you're stuck *and stressed*. Not good for your health—seriously. Another option at this point of stuckness is THC (delta-9-tetrahydrocannabinol), more popularly known as marijuana. The problem with this solution is threefold: one, while most forms of cannabis are psychoactive or mind-altering drugs, you may find yourself forgetting what the problem was in the first place. Two, your ability to problem-solve may be dramatically diminished. And three, you may develop anxiety and/or paranoia, believing in earnest that your client is actually CIA, KGB, or ET.

This leads us to another possible solution: cocaine. While this particular pharmaceutical may result in a brief sense of euphoria,

183

there is no guarantee that it will help you solve the creative problem at hand. You may, in fact, grow restless, irritable, and anxious. That, plus the known health effects of cocaine and its addictive properties, make it a less-than-ideal tool in the designer's toolbox. Which leads us, then, to methylenedioxymethamphetamine. In addition to its long and unpronounceable name (some opt to shorten it to "E"), ecstasy may produce a somewhat dreamlike state, but your productivity is likely to be hindered as you admire all the pretty new colors and attempt to seduce your husky HR person.

The other hallucinogen worth discussing here is lysergic acid diethylamide or LSD. This may be the most useful of all the available drugs simply because it generally causes you to see images, hear sounds, and feel sensations that seem real but aren't. Since your creative problem is very real, looking for this particular kind of miracle can be extremely counterproductive. Plus, most brand managers have a difficult time approving any creative solution that involves unicorns or bleeding clouds.

So, where does that leave our poor designers and their seemingly insurmountable creative obstacles? How are they supposed to break free from their doldrums? Where will the inspiration come from?

I would like to prescribe three other possible approaches:

1. Go back to the brief. Question every line. See if it squares with your own experience with the category or with this specific brand. Go to the "main takeaway" section (or whatever your firm's equivalent might be), and ask yourself if it resonates with you. If it doesn't, think of one to ten other ideas that do.

2. Rewrite the brief if you have to. Go visit the strategist or account person who generated the brief and put them on the spot. Challenge them to convince you of the main takeaway.

3. Develop a deeper relationship with the brand. Some people think I'm a little unhinged when I suggest that brands speak to us, but I'm convinced that they do. If you're working on a bicycle brand, go buy the bike or ask your client for one (the client will almost always oblige—even if you have to return it later). If you're working on a new package or ad campaign for a shampoo brand, get a bottle of that shampoo and set it on your desk. Pick it up and play with it. Use it. Rinse and repeat—repeatedly. If you're working on a brochure for a sports car, get up and go to the dealership, take an extended test drive, and don't forget to ask the salesperson to tell you why this car is better than a BMW or a Nissan.

4. Forget the assignment for a while. This is different from procrastinating and holding out for the last minute deadline energy boost because you're actually being proactive. Get out of your office and go to the nearest art museum or gallery or bowling alley. Push the problem out of your mind and just take in the inspiration that you find here. It will come back to you later—I promise. In certain cases, depending upon your project's deadline and the rest of your workload, I recommend playing hooky and seeing a movie. Not a mainstream blockbuster, necessarily, but one where art trumps box office. Again, I encourage you to submerge any concepts or connections to your project that you might want to make while you're watching it. It will all come back to you in spades when you get back to your studio.

If these measures don't help (and they almost always do), you may be in deep trouble. In which case, I highly recommend that you avail yourself of the minds and talents of the other people in your studio; tapping into the part of every creative person's brain that wants to be the hero, that wants to be the one who comes up with the final word to complete the crossword, will result in some extremely useful feedback.

David Ogilvy, in his classic piece of Ogilvy & Mather propaganda, *Ogilvy On Advertising*, actually recommends that writers sit down with a glass of Scotch when working on a project. While I have tremendous respect for a good glass of Scotch—and for Ogilvy's wit and taste—I question his methodology. I know it has worked for many other writers throughout history, with mixed results, but I would suggest a nonalcoholic alternative. Like a triple latte. Or (only in the gravest cases) Mountain Dew, Red Bull, or Rockstar. These tend to be less addictive, and if we know anything about the creative temperament, we know that addiction can be an issue.

In the final analysis, there are many healthy alternatives for creatives seeking an edge—especially when they hit the wall. The ones that I've enumerated here are just a few that I have found to be helpful. You probably have your own ways of dealing with stagnation and designer's block. But I would venture a guess that they include at least some of the techniques noted above (the nonmedicinal ones).

Clients and laymen alike think that we occasionally resort to illicit drugs, especially when our solutions are slightly more abstract or nonlinear. There is generally an atmosphere of "don't ask, don't tell," and I'm not suggesting here that we break the silence. If people want to believe that we drop acid in order to arrive at a radical creative solution, let them, as long as they can see all the hard work, logic, and effort we've expended to give them communications that resonate, inspire, and make the cash register ring. Because as far as clients are concerned, that's the headiest, most intoxicating thing of all.

WHAT WOULD HAPPEN IF I DID ~~A PIECE ON CURIOSITY?~~

5.0 MIN.

Recently, I received some feedback from one of my favorite designers regarding his need for any kind of outside stimulation. He said, "For me, there is so much excitement on any new project that I just dive into it," adding, "In my profession, there is never a dull moment." Poor kid. Obviously a junior designer fresh out of school. Full of all that charming idealism and naïve optimism that will no doubt get beaten out of him in the next year or two by duplicitous clients and internal politics. Except that these weren't the words of an upstart designer, but of someone who has been practicing design at the highest possible level since the Johnson administration.

As a follow-up to the chapter on appropriate drugs, I wanted to hook you up with something that ignites and fuels the imaginations of some of the top design and advertising practitioners in the world. I say this rather assertively, as if it were fact, but I'm really just being observant. The anecdotes are compelling, if not endless.

The legendary exuberance and enthusiasm of the aforementioned design god.

The founder of the global creative powerhouse who practically jumps out of bed every morning and has been known to randomly blurt out the words, "Isn't life fucking amazing?"

The storied West Coast designer who didn't know how much money he made, so when faced with a request for the details of his compensation, he had to go ask his business person, who jotted down the number on a Post-It note. The designer responded, "Holy crap! That's awesome!"

I could go on and on about some of the top figures in design and advertising—people who have been there. But, having been there, these creative leaders have not entirely lost their innocence, nor their excitement about getting to do what they love to do.

I would like to make two confessions.

Confession number one (and you have to promise not to share this with any of my clients): I still feel a bit guilty every time I get paid. The truth is, I would do 95 percent of what I do for free—I love it that much.

Confession two: I have just come through a set of challenging and unfortunate circumstances with a few key clients that resulted in two faulty beliefs, premises that threatened to strip every shred of optimism and joy from my working life. Those beliefs could be summarized by two axioms that I found myself repeating far too regularly: "There are a million ways to die," and "Clients are guilty until proven innocent." The first premise obviously refers to the attachment one develops to those rare and hard-won ideas and the gauntlet the ideas have to run to see the light of day. The emotional roller-coaster ride of pushing yourself to find a meaningful creative solution only to see it die at the hands of mid-level managers for all the wrong reasons. Or some other equally effective implement of torture. Which then led quite naturally to the second conclusion, that clients are essentially "bad."

I said that I "have just come through" this rather dark and depressing valley of my career. Maybe you'd be curious to know how I eventually "came through" it. Well, exposure to the positivism of some of the individuals mentioned above definitely helped, but ultimately, it came down to a decision I had to make: to return to the almost childlike wonder of getting to do what I love to do. I had to decide that it is worth it: worth the disappointments, worth the frustrations—worth everything, just to create one Cranium WOW package. To conceive one Beigeland print ad. To launch one Wordstock outdoor campaign. Even to simply contribute to the brand voice and identity for a Skylab Architecture Web site or a decent headline for a Kettle Chips ad or a semi-inspiring manifesto that gets the founders of a start-up investment firm all frothy and ready to take on the world. My work makes everything else tolerable.

That's the first breakthrough. The second is one of the most powerful principles that I have ever stumbled onto in my career. It almost makes me want to go on the road and do motivational seminars or some other annoying thing like that. (Think Tom Cruise in *Magnolia*.) Here it is: curiosity. That's it. One word. But it makes all the difference in a meeting when I am convinced of the rightness of a particular direction but things seem to be going another way. Austin + passion + assertiveness—*without curiosity*—just comes off as aggressiveness or worse: bossiness or rigidity. I'm labeled "difficult" at this point. And that's accurate. But Austin + passion + assertiveness + CURIOSITY opens everything up. I'm not so entrenched, and almost magically, the room becomes less entrenched, as well. I can ask good questions, explore alternatives, and trust my colleagues and even (God forbid) the client. Defensiveness disappears on both sides of the argument, and the argument is no longer an argument, but a discussion. No, an *exploration*.

Last week, one of my favorite designers and I were presenting two different campaign directions to a client. One of the directions was considerably more challenging than the other—a genuine departure for the category. We trusted the work. We trusted each other. We trusted

191

the client. And the client's comment surprised (and heartened) all of us. He said, "I like the one that makes the consumer have to think and figure it out."

It reminds me of the mantra that Antonio Pierce repeated to himself when his New York Giants upset the New England Patriots: "Let the game come to you." This requires trusting. Trusting the work. Trusting your colleagues. Trusting your clients. Ultimately, trusting the process. And by simply injecting a modicum of curiosity into the equation, a small miracle occurs. Everyone in that room—providing their soul is still somewhat intact—remembers:

We are getting to do what we love to do. And in our profession, there is truly never a dull moment.

193

WRITING AS ART

5.5 MIN.

I have my own nifty little criterion for evaluating art. Try it on and see if it fits:

"Art" is the intersection of craft and self-awareness.

That's it.

Now, art critics and academicians would probably roll their collective eyes at such a simplistic view. But, after years of curious reading, thinking, discussion, and debate, this has proven to be a pretty reliable decoder ring.

Think about the evolution of art through its various periods. Throughout the Renaissance, baroque, and romantic periods, and even well into the impressionist era, "great art" was all about craft and little else. If you didn't possess the requisite technical skills and your art didn't convey a certain realism—whether you were creating a portrait, a landscape, or a still life—you simply would not have been taken seriously as an artist. And probably with good reason. The cost of entry was a modicum of knowledge, competence, and technique, and while innovation and imagination can be seen in the art of these periods (and, in fact, was probably the underlying factor that separated the good artists from the great ones), artists were more or less standing naked with nothing but their technical skills—or the lack thereof—showing for everyone to see. It wasn't really until the last part of the nineteenth century and the first part of the twentieth that artists began to really question the canons of what constituted "art," and experimentation became acceptable. Guys like Cézanne, Toulouse-Lautrec, Velázquez, and El Greco may have greased the skids, but it was Picasso and Braque (both possessing prodigious technical skills, as evidenced in many of their earlier works)

195

who really kicked down the door not just to cubism, but to a whole new art universe, a universe where the Duchamps, the Warhols, the Dalís, the Pollocks, the Hirsts, the Emins, and so many others have challenged the very definition and essence of what art is.

This is where it gets good, because if you look at the development of art throughout history and the development and education of any modern or contemporary artist, you can see a direct parallel: craft, followed by a more abstract personal expression. Or, more to my point: craft, followed by self-awareness. It's almost like art as an entity needed to start out with craft (knowledge, training, technique, and skill) before it was able to veer off that crafty path into the uncharted territory of experimentation and even of self-reference and parody (Warhol, Hirst, Emin, Riswold, et al). Therein lies the difference between an original Jackson Pollock and an accident in a hardware store; between Damien Hirst and a taxidermist; between Tracey Emin's unmade bed and my own. They started out developing their knowledge, techniques, and skills—their craft. And over time, they developed their own unique and distinctive points of view—which, I would argue, are all about self-awareness. If you and I were to splash paint all over a canvas or put an animal in a vitrine or display our messy beds in a gallery, we might be able to pull it off with skill equal to theirs, but our efforts would lack self-awareness. There would be *art*-awareness, but people would (rightly) say, "Oh, they just ripped off Pollock or Hirst or Emin." Because those were *their* unique, intensely personal points of view, not ours.

When it comes to writing as art, I think there needs to be a certain level of craft before you can even begin to express yourself with any degree of self-awareness. That said, there are a lot of writers who may have the craft of writing down, but who are not necessarily creating art, simply because they lack that self-awareness and insight. I just finished *Demons* by Fyodor Dostoevsky. Throughout the book, his craft is flawless. Amazing. His characterizations are incredible, unparalleled in literature. But, with the exception of the raw and devastating "At Tikhon's," which was conspicuously cut from the original manuscript by his publisher, I think that *Crime and Punishment* and *The Brothers Karamazov* are more "artful" than *Demons*, in the sense that they feel far more personal and less doctrinaire. You keep finding yourself going, "I've totally felt that!" or, "I've totally thought that!"

I admit that I am not a big fan of modern fiction, but based on this criteria, current writers who seem to move from craft to a unique personal expression are authors like Chuck Palahniuk, David Sedaris, and Alice Sebold.

Other artists whom I think wrote with craft and self-awareness:

Milton

Somo guy named Shakespeare

St. Augustine

Cervantes

Melville

Emerson (he's the one who said that genius is believing that what is true for you in your inmost heart is true for everyone: self-awareness)

197

Dickens

Hugo (compare the craft in his descriptions of the natural world in *The Toilers of the Sea* with the powerful emotions he evokes in *Les Misérables* and *The Man Who Laughs*)

Thoreau

Frost

T.S. Eliot

Tolstoy

Rand (Ayn, not Paul; she slips in and out of art whenever she gets on her objectivist soapbox)

Hemingway (obviously—who else has inspired annual contests to see who can write like them?)

Salinger

Steinbeck

Fitzgerald

Orwell

Nietzsche

Tolkien

Lewis

Chandler

Kerouac (what made *On the Road* the testament of an entire generation if not his gravitas to assume that the mundane details of his life, told well and honestly, would be a work of art?)

Ginsberg

Burroughs

William Manchester (as biographers go, he seems to be huge on craft and bigger than most in terms of personal expression or a point of view, which puts him in the "artist" category for me)

Art seems to favor personal expression over craft; that's how you get a Jimi Hendrix, who couldn't read music but somehow developed his own particular kind of craft almost entirely based on his own personal expression, his inimitable "voice."

Maybe the compulsion to say something intensely personal is what drives people to develop their craft.

Maybe there's hope for those of us who feel that we might have something to say. Maybe that will force us to refine our craft. Maybe when we do, we will become more than craftspeople; maybe we will become artists.

MY ROLE IN ALL OF THIS

5.0 MIN.

Approximately once a week, I am asked something along the lines of, "Why are you so obsessed with design when your background is in advertising?" My answer is always something along the lines of, "The two worlds need to fuse." I'm as convinced of that as I am that I need to breathe. I have always had a bit of an inordinate interest in graphic and industrial design, as well as architecture, but over the past five years, I have grown in my conviction that the future of branded communications is in the fusion of advertising and design (and other brand-related disciplines) at a cellular level and not merely as an add-on, i.e., ad agencies doing more logos and design firms doing more ads. No, it really has to be something deeper and more disruptive—a top-to-bottom reassessment of the creative process, an allocation of human resources, and education.

As most of you are no doubt aware, it's already happening in various corners of the business. Wieden has John Jay and Todd Waterbury; Anomaly has Mike Byrne (and Dasani, thanks to equal parts smoke, mirrors, and genuine fusion); Taxi has Jane Hope; M&C Saatchi was smart enough to bring in Peter Saville to infect its entire culture. Of the experiment, the fifty-one-year-old maverick designer said, "Things have changed significantly over the last ten years in the wake of the convergence culture. There's a much greater shared language between the two disciplines now." A much greater shared language, sure, but for the most part, that's where the sharing ends. The fusion, or "convergence culture," as Saville frames it, must go beyond language. That's what I mean by "cellular level" versus "add-on."

I learned last week that one of the top design practices on the West Coast completed a year-long restructuring of top management with

201

the appointments of a senior account manager and a senior account planner, both from very traditional advertising agencies. This move can't help but have a huge impact on the firm's internal systems and processes and, ultimately, the projects they bring in and their overall creative output. These are smart folks. They see something. They see fusion.

One of my favorite designers turned me onto a book by Pieter Brattinga, a designer, educator, and impresario. The cover alone would have been worth the $40 I shelled out for it on Abe Books (*www.abebooks.com*). But the title was so dry and innocuous that I had pretty much chalked this volume up to "one of those beautiful books that I never actually get around to reading." The title: *Planning for Industry, Art, and Education.* Fortunately, though, I did get around to reading this gem. A piece written by Dutch poet and writer Simon Vinkenoog did a better job of answering the weekly question about my twin passions for design and advertising than I could have ever done myself. Check it out:

> *The man who objectively follows and records the course of many events for the sole purpose of benefiting himself and his fellow men is a new type of human being: he acts as a communication expert or mediator between people and groups, between interests and needs. A new human being who helps to shape the future by taking a constructive part in building the present. It is not merely a matter of efficiency—although the release of manpower implies the possibility of using human intellect elsewhere in creating new projects.*

> *The mediator "surmises" because he has specialized in gathering knowledge transcending all disciplines and enabling him to gain*

insight from everyday practice; thanks to observation, his conjectures can be verified. For is not whatever he finds open to inspection by anyone who may be interested?

The mediator often succeeds in reestablishing, restoring a long-lost contact (advertising and design as practiced by Paul Rand, George Lois, and others). His is the view of an outsider within a given structure, a routine, a setup—and his practiced eye recognizes, because it sees for the first time, the flaws escaping those who have become used to them day by day without being capable of tracing them to their source. He can test his theories in actual practice.

He is uncommitted; he does not represent any organization, and is only obliged to choose when offered the opportunity of examining all aspects of a given problem. He is without bias, unless it is a question of taking action—any action—against stagnancy in the form of apathy, fear, shortsightedness.

Much work is done at cross-purposes; much energy is wasted because men pore over problems that have already been solved.

The mediator is the man who gives shape to his curiosity by being alert to whatever he may still be able to accomplish. He does not sit back and wait, but keeps knocking on the door. His speech is direct and confined to essentials. He penetrates to the core of things and does not let himself be taken in by appearances.

What I like best is to work out ideas; mankind has them by the myriad waiting to be picked up and used. When we come together, there is bound to be mutual inspiration.

My response when I first read these words and when I reread them now: holy freaking crap. This was written in 1970, decades before a "convergence culture" was even a twinkle in the eye of John Jay or Todd Waterbury or Mike Byrne or Jane Hope or Peter Saville. Thirty-five years before I began writing a book on the necessary but unlikely fusion of advertising and graphic design, before I began consulting with design firms and helping them rebrand themselves as hybrid creative companies. Before I knew that there was a name for what I was doing quite naturally.

I'm a "mediator" and I didn't even know it. And now, thanks to a few paragraphs by an obscure Dutch writer in an even more obscure book, I have a brief for my career.

THE END

0.5 MIN.

INDEX

6.0 MIN.

Index

APPENDIX

8.5 MIN.

Gold Stars

Appendix

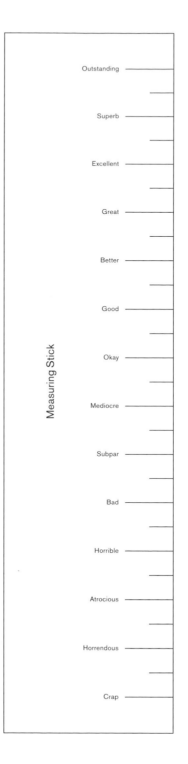

Dog Ear

217

Left-handed Scissors

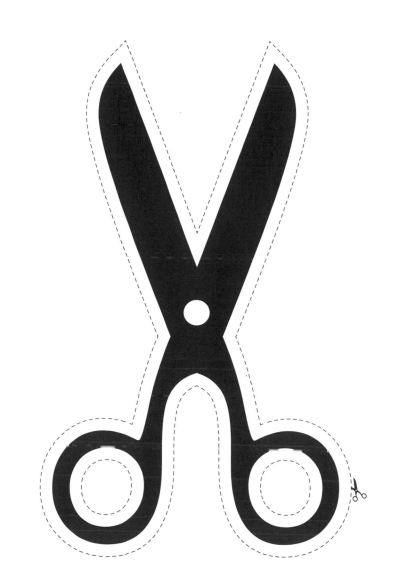

Right-handed Scissors

THISISWHEREISTOPPEDREADING

Books from Allworth Press

Corporate Creativity: Developing an Innovative Organization
edited by Thomas Lockwood and Thomas Walton (6"x 9", 256 pages, paperback, 100 b&w illustrations, $24.95)

AIGA Professional Practices in Graphic Design, Second Edition
edited by Tad Crawford (6"x 9", 320 pages, paperback, $29.95)

Green Graphic Design
by Brian Dougherty with Celery Design Collaborative (6"x 9", 212 pages, paperback, 100 b&w illustrations, $19.95)

How to Think Like a Great Graphic Designer
by Debbie Millman (6"x 9", 256 pages, paperback, $24.95)

Design Disasters: Great Designers, Fabulous Failures, and Lessons Learned
edited by Steven Heller (6"x 9", 240 pages, paperback, $24.95)

Building Design Strategy: Using Design to Achieve Key Business Objectives
edited by Thomas Lockwood and Thomas Walton (6"x 9", 272 pages, paperback, $24.95)

Creating the Perfect Design Brief: How to Manage Design for Strategic Advantage
by Peter L. Phillips (6"x 9", 224 pages, paperback, $19.95)

Designing Logos: The Process of Creating Logos That Endure
by Jack Gernsheimer (8.5"x 10", 208 pages, paperback, $35.00)

The Graphic Designer's Guide to Better Business Writing
by Barbara Janoff and Ruth Cash-Smith (6"x 9", 256 pages, paperback, $19.95)

The Graphic Design Business Book
by Tad Crawford (6"x 9", 256 pages, paperback, $24.95)

Business and Legal Forms for Graphic Designers, Third Edition
by Tad Crawford and Eva Doman Bruck (8.5"x 11", 208 pages, paperback, includes CD-ROM, $29.95)

The Graphic Designer's Guide to Pricing, Estimating, and Budgeting, Revised Edition
by Theo Stephan Williams (6.75" × 9.875", 208 pages, paperback, $19.95)

The Graphic Designer's Guide to Clients: How to Make Clients Happy and Do Great Work
by Ellen Shapiro (6"x 9", 256 pages, paperback, $19.95)

Editing by Design: For Designers, Art Directors, and Editors
by Jan V. White (8.5"x 11", 256 pages, paperback, $29.95)

To request a free catalog or order books by credit card, call 1-800-491-2808. To see our complete catalog on the World Wide Web, or to order online for a 20 percent discount, you can find us at *www.allworth.com*.